Words to HER

Postpartum stories for Mommies

Naviane Collier

And

Mothers

Words to Her: Postpartum Stories for Mommies
Naviane Collier

ISBN: 979-8-9879164-1-4

Dedicated to:

Every single woman, soon to be mommies, postpartum mommies, and all mothers. This book is written to inspire, uplift, and give postpartum mommies a voice.

Table of Contents

Acknowledgments

My name may be on the cover of this book, but by no means was this masterpiece created by myself. There are many mothers and a father who had a hand in making this book all that it is. There have also been several key people that supported, listened, and have given advice. They all deserve acknowledgment and gratitude, starting with:

My Lord, Jesus Christ, thank you for giving me this idea to carry forth.

Dr. Kimberly O. Packer: FLOW Write Publishing thank you for taking on this project.

My Husband: Gabriel Collier your love and support is unmatched.

My Son: Roman Collier, you taught me consistency during difficult times.

My Mother: Noel Robertson, thank you for your endless example of perseverance

My Mother-in-Law: Carrier Collier, thank you for your raw example of love

Contributing Authors - thank you for saying yes:
Lexxus Betts Keyes
Morgan Taylor-McFadden
Nigerain Collier
Dynika Marshall
Rodneshia Seals
Quantisha Oliver
Amber D. Brown-Jones
Mary K Purnell MS, MBA
Whitney Moody
Shana Middleton
Luwanna Randle
Kelly Morris-Jordan
Jessica N Monroe

Introduction

For many of us, once we finally get our "Big Fat Positive" pregnancy results, a feeling of excitement and anxiety overtake our bodies. We beam with joy because our bodies can create life how God intended. We fill our minds and homes with things that pertain to the little bundle of joy that is soon coming. We have appointment after appointment ensuring that the little one will come into this world healthy and safe. For nine months, these little bundles are receiving top notch care and attention. As the pregnancy comes to an end and our bodies move into labor and delivery, we receive tons of attention from medical professionals. They're coaching us through one of the toughest and rewarding experiences our bodies will ever go through. On that beautiful day, we miraculously bring forth new life into this world.

Depending on your birthing story, we spend the next few days and/or weeks receiving care for our little ones and ourselves. Then, the strangest thing happens, they let you take a whole baby home alone. WHAT?? WHY??? Please come home with me, I am not ready to be alone with this tiny baby. Just joking. But seriously! All jokes aside…they allow you to take a baby home without anyone confirming your home or life is setup to care for such a special gift. We get little to no direction on how to care for our babies and ourselves once discharged from the hospital, or wherever you deliver your tiny human.

I remember my husband and I bringing our baby into our apartment and laying him on the bed. I took one look at our baby boy and knew our lives would forever be changed. Sitting there looking at him with my eyes welling up with tears of joy and anxiety, I was praying for God to guide me through this motherhood journey. Once the high of excitement and anxiety began to settle and the painkillers started wearing off, I felt like I was just hit by a car. I walked into our bathroom, took off my nightgown and looked at my body in the mirror.

I had so many questions, intrusive thoughts, and sadness about my body. I started wondering would I be one of the women that "snap back" after pregnancy. How long will I have to tolerate this pain that is overtaking my body. I started feeling like everything was closing in on me and the world was just dropped on my shoulders. I kept thinking to myself, "Girly, you only got six weeks until you are over this postpartum period". My goodness was I so freaking wrong. After doing some research, I found that there is no set time frame for the postpartum period. It can range from six weeks to whenever o'clock. I struggle with postpartum rage, intrusive thoughts, mood swings, and self-grief for six months. I looked online to find information and read some books around women's experiences with postpartum. I found little to no information that could explain to me what was going on with me. I felt so lost and alone; unsure how long these feeling would last. Well, I am going to pause right here because you'll read more of my experience in the upcoming chapter.

I felt alone in my postpartum journey and decided I didn't want other mommies to feel the way I did. As I began to have the conversation, I found that even in my small circle, there were others who were eager to share their postpartum journeys, too. My vision for this wonderfully crafted masterpiece is to uplift, inspire, and educate any mommy or soon-to-be mommy. I want you to know you are not alone and there are other mommies who understand your story and can relate to what you are going through. Please continue reading to learn from some outstanding mommies.

Chapter 1

Stages of Self-Grief

Lead Author: Naviane Collier

Grief is the anguish experienced after significant loss,
usually the death of a beloved person.
Merriam-Webster online

All of us have experience some level of grief in our lives. Can you imagine being in a consistent state of grief for two years? If not, allow me to take you on my journey through loss, birth, self-grief, and acceptance throughout pregnancy and postpartum. Imagine this common scene on TV and/or movie where a person is hearing a lot of thoughts going on in their mind and then they begin screaming. That was me screaming on the inside wondering when this nightmare would end. I am not a person who talks about my personal hardship but, I do believe this will help a mommy in a similar situation. If that mommy is you, I pray you will find comfort in my short story.

The year 2021 will be a year I will never forget. In 2021, my husband and I both agree and felt in our spirit that we should try for a baby. Yay! At that time, we were heading in to our ninth year of marriage. We waited long enough. So, we jumped in headfirst, and we hit a home run on our first try. My goodness this must be

God! Right? Come with me as I paint this picture of what our lives looked like at this time.

First, I just took a leap of faith into entrepreneurship, and it was not going well. Then, we lost my husband's grandmother. We most definitely needed a win, and we felt this was our win. We started looking for an OBGYN and found one we liked. She scheduled our appointment during my tenth week of pregnancy. Great! My mother was coming into town the same day as the appointment. We planned to "pop" the news once she got to our home. Those ten weeks felt like it was dragging by so freaking slowly. Girl! The big day finally came, and I had so many questions around this prenatal checkup. Our physician began the pelvic exam and our little one popped on the screen. My husband and I both looked at each other smiling from ear to ear. The room felt so still for the next few moments. Then, our physician said, "I can't find the heartbeat". The doctor's voice was so very distant, and it felt as if she didn't have empathy behind her words. Her first suggestion was to terminate the pregnancy. What? No way! My head began to spin, and I couldn't hold the tears back at this point. Why would she want me to kill my baby? She then said, "you all can see if anything changes in two weeks". It was a lot to process and of course, my husband and I opted to wait the two weeks. As I write this, it's difficult for me to recall the details without tears flowing from my eyes. My objective is not to scary you, Momma, but to let you know the sun will always come out tomorrow.

Now, don't forget we had to pick up my mother from the airport within the next couple of hours. We headed home and I felt so lifeless. I couldn't for the life of me understand why God would allow us to go through this. We picked my mother up from the airport and I put on the bravest face I could. We finally made it back home and my mother began to talk about everything that was going on with her. Then, my sister texted that her and her family were heading over to our house. I just couldn't hold the tears back any longer and I spilled the beans to my mother. My mother had never experienced a situation like this before and didn't know how to comfort me. We ended up having a huge falling out during her visit. I viewed it as another hit to the chest. My business failed, my husband's grandmother passed, the doctor couldn't find the heartbeat, and now my mother and I are not on speaking terms. God please! I need a win, Lord! Just as if I had said the opposite, we were told we had to go with the D&C because the baby stopped growing. Then, July came around (my birthday month), and my sister texted me to say she had some news for me. She was pregnant with my beautiful niece. I had to muster up some joy to pour into her, even though I was still lifeless inside.

My world was crashing down before my eyes. I decided to go see a therapist to help with everything that was happening. During my sessions I had to relive everything all over again. Plus, I had to come to terms that I never really grieved my father passing. My life felt like a huge dark cloud was following me with no sign of sunshine. I kept feeling like I was hanging from a cliff, holding on with one hand. I am not here telling you all this to highlight the negative events in my life, but to encourage you to keep holding on. When you hold fast and not give up this is what I promise you: peace, understanding, and strength.

As the year 2021 was transitioning out, I couldn't be happier. But it seemed like it couldn't leave without more disappointment. We started trying again for a little one: November, not pregnant and December, not pregnant. Then, the last two weeks of the year, I got the news that my cousin passed away, and my aunt has stage four cancer. All around me seemed like a stench of grief engulfing me. I just had no clue what to do but continue holding on to **FAITH** which felt impossible at times.

Hello January! Cheers to 2022, can you say it with me 2022! We finally got our "Big Fat Positive" result on January 19, 2022. Seeing the positive pregnancy result brought a wave of excitement and fear into my heart. I told myself not to get fully attach just yet, wait until the doctor's appointment to ensure everything's on track.

We scheduled the pelvic exam during my fifth week of pregnancy, and we heard the heartbeat. That wave came right back: excitement and fear. My mind wouldn't allow me to surrender to happiness. I asked my OBGYN if we could schedule an appointment during my eighth week. This appointment was slightly different. She didn't let us hear the heartbeat, but we saw the flickering of the heartbeat and saw our baby moving. Can you guess by now what happened next? Correct! That same freaking wave excitement and fear. I couldn't get out of my head. I just kept thinking about all the loss I experienced last year.

Grief still had a hold of me, and the wave of bad news just kept coming. During the second month of my pregnancy, my

.er had her beautiful baby girl, and my aunt with stage four cancer passed on the same day. Then, a few days later my husband got the news his first cousin passed. Anxiety and fear took residence and followed me most of my pregnancy, which caused me to go into a slight depression. If you are experiencing any type of loss during your pregnancy, please take care of yourself by surrounding yourself with loving and kindhearted people you trust. My husband was my support system during our pregnancy. We had no family or friends close by due to us moving to Houston, TX. We both worked from home which was an absolute blessing.

I want to switch gears and give you some things that helped me during this time. It's important to me that you relate to my story. But it's more important that you leave with some tools to help you on your journey. **Tip number 1:** I listened to a gospel song that ministered to my soul every morning (Draw Me Close to You by Marvin Winans). **Tip number 2:** I ate super healthy and drank tons of water most of my pregnancy (mostly fruits and veggies). **Tip number 3:** I got a lot of rest (if your baby or other littles ones allow you). **Tip number 4:** I got outside to walk as much as possible, or I did very light workouts (Youtuber GrowwithJo or my husband trilo_gfitness). **Tip number 5:** I met with my therapist once a month to talk about the fears I was having around the pregnancy. I want you all to know I had a wonderful pregnancy even with all the loss and fear that surrounded me. Our baby boy took it so easy on his mommy most of the time. I do understand that most pregnancies are not like this. I can only encourage you to take it easy on yourself and find ten minutes a day for **yourself!**

Now, jumping back into the next phase…Hello, Postpartum! October 5, 2023, we brought home our wonderful baby boy with excitement and uncertainty. Looking at our baby boy on the bed in his car seat oblivious of what's lying head. If you ever seen a scary movie, you can recall the scene where the person is home alone just going about their day as normal. Then, out of nowhere, chaos. That is how postpartum sneaks up on you, silent but deadly.

Yes, I do watch a ton of movies. It's one of my favorite hobbies. I told some of my postpartum experience in the introduction so let's pick it up there. I thought I would have my beautiful baby and pop back into who I was. This is what you call a lack of knowledge, and our first stage of self-grief, denial (ignorance) on my behalf.

Denial is a defense mechanism that individuals use to reject reality. Well, I refused to listen to my husband when he kept asking me, "what's something you want to do for yourself after we have our baby?" He would say, "think about what you want to do and pick a day once a week you would like to have". I kept saying to myself, he's being so freaking extra. I know how to think for myself and how to get out the house when I want to. Ladies! I was so freaking wrong; I should've listened to what he was trying to convey. Once you bring that little bundle of joy home, your life is forever changed. If you don't have a plan in place to help you put yourself first, you will lose yourself. For a lot of mommies, you're okay with giving all of yourself to your precious baby. I am here

11

.ell you you're doing more harm than good. You cannot pour from an empty cup, and that's what's going to happen. I may have rub some of you the wrong way just now. But, I am only telling you this to help you save yourself, your baby, and your relationship if you are in one.

During the first month after having our baby, I wanted to prove to everyone (cough no one knew I was doing this) that I could handle everything. I wanted to show them that I am **SUPERWOMAN** not necessarily superwoman, but something like her. I pushed myself and pushed myself to take care of our baby, the house, and be supportive to my husband. My mother came for a month to help us transition into parenthood. I even wanted to show her that I didn't really need her help (but thanks for coming). When I felt pain, I pushed it to the back of my mind because I didn't have time for that. I had to show them that I knew how to juggle and support everyone and myself because this is what mothers do. RIGHT? Listen! I was in utter denial; I would go as far to call it delusional. All I can do right now is shake my head in shame. If I could do it all over again, I would let go of control and be totally open for help. I didn't let go of control because I needed something to hold on to. All the loss I experienced would not allow me to release control and accept the help. By not letting go I became extremely angry.

Anger is a completely natural emotion. We all experience being angry one time or another. Where anger can become dangerous is when you sit in it too long and become enraged. I am thankful that I didn't allow my anger to take me that far. I did experience a deep level of anger towards myself, my husband, and my life. As I mentioned, I wanted to be **SUPERWOMAN** and that came at a huge cost since I am only **HUMAN**. With the strains of motherhood: breastfeeding, sleepless nights, crying, plus wifely duties, and trying to pack to move, I started losing a piece of myself day after day without even noticing. One of the worst days I can recall was when my son wouldn't let up crying, and he wouldn't go to my husband. Plus, we had to finish packing since our lease was coming to an end. My lovely husband and I waited to the very last minute to begin packing. I didn't have a chance to wash myself, brush my teeth, and I barely ate that day. I felt overwhelmed, pissed, and overworked. But, keep in mind, I allowed myself to become overworked by not giving up control. The control I was trying to hold on to was slipping away along with losing myself. I would look in the mirror and not even acknowledge myself because I didn't know who was staring back at me.

I became angry at everything because it felt cruel and unfair that a woman should lose her body, mind, soul, health, and so much more. Whereas our loved ones seem free as a bird, and we're the caged bird. When I would see my husband eat, workout, laugh, wash, step out for a second (let's just say do anything that appeared like he was unrestricted), I became furious. I would say to myself how in the heck does he has time to do "x, y, and z". Just talking to myself in my head like, "I know he can see me and smell me. I am the one breastfeeding, stressed, packing this apartment, and trying to heal". I can see how much I endorsed my negative emotions and overlooked my reality. My husband would plead with me to take some time for myself, and I would get angry whenever he mentioned it. I wanted him to take a real hard look at what I am doing and see if he could find free time. I didn't want help, I wanted him to feel like I felt. I know this doesn't sound right but I am only telling you this to help you see how postpartum can alter our way of thinking and seeing things.

Day after day I would authorize my inner thoughts to torment my mind and the way I saw my life. This steered me into anxiety, which turned into depression. The Bible mentions that anxiety can produce depression. I witnessed this firsthand when I realize that I lost another person, **MYSELF**. The more I tried to control my life, the more life took away from me. I went from denial to anger, and now I was sitting in depression. The depression stage really tormented me. I would go from sadness to weeping, weeping to denial, denial to "zombie-ness". This cycle kept repeating day after day, hour after hour, and sometimes minute after minute. My mind would take me to some dark places, and I would just begin crying. I wanted my old life back along with who I was. I knew I could never get those things back (thank God) which caused me to overeat and gain fifteen pounds, breakout all over my body, become a hermit, and have malicious thoughts. When you are going through depression, you forget the people you love. I mismanaged my relationships', including my marriage, friendships, and immediate family.

What started to shake the ground from under me was hearing a ton of people committing suicide, and I knew I had to do something about my inner thoughts and life before I became next. My thoughts and the words that were coming out of my mouth were all toxic. I would try and cover up my thoughts and emotions to keep appearing to others like I had it all together. Once I knew I had to step into this new level of life, I had to give up the control. I couldn't bear the weight. It wasn't mine in the first place. This unlocked an inner peace which helped me to accept the "now". This drives me to my last stage of Self-Grief: Acceptance.

Acceptance: being able to accept the reality of what's happening and beginning to look for avenues to move forward toward the mark. Coming into the realization that my circumstance can only change once I let go of control and shift my mindset. The enemy (inner me) was stealing my happiness, peace, joy, and life. I kept bruising myself repeatedly by speaking harshly to myself and body. I felt like I was being pulled down into a sink hole, crying out to the Lord to save little me. I kept eating and sleeping my feelings away to suppress the hurt and shame. Being far away from friends and family caused me and my husband to carry the weight alone. If you're tackling motherhood alone, I pray that God provides you the grace to continue and bring you a community to uplift you.

You may be saying to yourself, so what did you do to arrive to acceptance? **First**, I had to be real with myself about my circumstances and ask God to help me change the things that I could not. I started with drinking enough water to cleanse my insides and changed the way I was eating (started this process all over again fruits and veggies). **Second**, I challenged myself to take a walk at least two or three times a week. Before my baby, I weighed around 130 pounds. After having my baby, I was 19 pounds heavier. This really effected my emotional state, because I couldn't fit into my old clothes, and I didn't feel sexy. So, I decided to walk. I knew walking has tons of benefits that would help me lose the weight and feel better. Walking can strengthen bones, reduce excess body fat, and boost muscle power and endurance just to name a few benefits. **Third**, I reached out to different mommies I knew and asked them to tell me the things they wish they knew about postpartum. This helped me to see that I was not the only one going through this. **Fourth**, I let go of control by communicating to my husband about my thoughts, emotions, and telling him what I needed in that season. **Lastly**, I started speaking life into myself as much as possible and getting out the house. I had to stop rejecting my situation and body if I wanted complete healing. I am not fully where I want to be, but I am nowhere near where I was. I thank God every day for the transformation that happened within. I am now able to pull away from the baby and "wifey" duties to spend time with **ME**.

I want you to know that you're stronger than those thoughts and your body will only surrender once you give yourself grace. Take it one day at a time by taking super small steps until you can handle more, and you develop consistency and discipline. Lastly, I want to tell you how proud I am of you. You picked up this book to find answers and I hope you find them within these pages. Much Love, Mommy!

To my husband, thank you for being everything and more to me and our family. Roman and I love you dearly and you're an amazing husband and father.

Chapter 2

Mommy Shuffle

Lexxus Betts Keyes

My mother always told me that if you want to make God laugh, tell him all the plans you have for your life. In my early 20's, I aspired to be a wife and mother. Many may think I set these goals for myself because I wanted to be like everyone else: have kids before 30 in order to still be able to live my life in my 50's, have "simple pregnancies" with less risks, or be able to have an amazing "snap back". It was quite the contrary for me. I have always been in tuned with my body, my family's medical history and what signs to look out for when it comes to health and safety. One thing I knew for sure is that thyroids, diabetes and erratical menstrual cycles run in my family.

During my freshman year of college, I began having inconclusive paps smear where I was being monitored every six months for signs of cancer and thyroid issues. My world completely changed after that first inconclusive test. Every six months, I was traveling back and forth from North Carolina where I was attending school to Indianapolis, Indiana, which is my hometown. Since the doctors knew my family history and three generations of us still living in Indianapolis, I felt more comfortable making the trips to meet with the physicians. I remember sitting down that day and physically writing out everything that I wanted in a husband, when I wanted to have children, the number of children I wanted, and I even had the nerve to have names picked out.

At 20 years old, I thought my life was completely mapped out. My priority list was as follows: graduate with a degree in Biomedical Engineering, accept an offer prior to graduation for full time employment, get married and begin having children by 25. I know I humored God so much because the details were in the pudding, and I did not even know the flavor.

Fast forward to my 25th birthday, I was working as a Quality Engineer, single and starting a business. Out of everything on my priority list, there was only one thing I had marked off the list and that was the full-time offer in my dream position. I still thank God for that! I began to lose faith in a lot of things. I was still having inconclusive pap smears, I began having menstrual migraines, and just knew the clock I placed on myself had ran out. I begin to replace all the negative thoughts and bury myself in my work and business. I was obsessed with staying busy so my mind would not be idle. I became so busy that I was losing sight of life itself. I remember talking with my bestie-cousin about how I was feeling, and in her best fashion she said you should be doing you like I am doing me.

Starting the summer of 2019, I did just that. I began to travel almost every month, worked extremely hard on my day job, took a position over the African American Professional Network at my company, and was still running an Event Management business.

Life was going great, and I was so busy with everything else that the fears I had about marriage, pregnancy and other health concerns went out of the window.

It wasn't until the start of the pandemic that I had to slow down and just sit. During this time of isolation, I reconnected with one of my best guy friends from my alma mater of North Carolina A&T State University. We were both student athletes, both STEM students and both about our business. We had always supported one another in our endeavors, but never seemed to have time to really stop and hang out for long periods of time. After he completed his professional career in Arena Football, he settled in the small city of Greenville, North Carolina and closed on a property. I was extremely proud of him that a week later I drove up from Raleigh, North Carolina to congratulate him and bring a housewarming gift. We sat and talked for hours. Then, we went over to his parents who still lived in their hometown about 40 minutes away, and played spades. For the first time, we had an opportunity to just sit down and breathe a bit. Two young, black, intelligent folks who were busy-bodies being forced to sit down due to the pandemic. Little did we know how great that was for us. After the housewarming weekend, we began dating through the pandemic and life was great. I began having those thoughts again about marriage and children. After two years of dating, things were getting serious. I started looking online at engagement rings that I liked and sending hints on Instagram. We then began talking about having children two years after marriage, and really were on a path to travel the world for a bit.

In November of 2022, I was traveling home for Thanksgiving break and met up with old friends and my family. I had plans to have a great time. The night before Thanksgiving, I was extremely sick. I could not hold food down and my demeanor was extremely off. I just knew it was COVID. I began freaking out. I prayed asking God to give me guidance on what I should do, because I did not want to get anyone else sick. That evening, I went to sleep, and God revealed to me in a vivid dream that I was going to be a mother. I saw myself in the hospital bed surrounded by my current boyfriend and my mother. The dream felt so real. I woke up laughing because I knew that was not possible because I hadn't had a missed cycle or anything. I dismissed it and tried to finish enjoying my Thanksgiving break with family. However, I was still not feeling well and had to cut my time short with family just to rest. After four days of doubting the dream, I took a pregnancy test and the dream was confirmed, I was pregnant.

My world started to spin. This was not as planned. Denzel (my boyfriend) had not proposed yet, we still had our two-year plan, and we both were still athletes and working and doing a lot of extracurricular activities. How can I also handle the pressure of being a mom and we live in two different cities? My usual Lexxus shuffle, hustle and bustle of a lifestyle would come to a halt with a baby on the way, and there were so many pieces to the puzzle to figure out. The immediate questions that began to surface in my brain were: What will Mommy Lexx's lifestyle look like? Growing up as an only child, would I struggle with sharing time and space? Am I going to be a great mother like my mom is for me?

The planner in me began doing what I normally do and started mapping out a plan. I thought, God revealed the pregnancy to me in a dream, and now it was time to plan and execute! Oh, how wrong I was. In these moments, God wanted to me to remain in my reflective period. Instead, I was Lexx, the hustler, with a growing baby. The hustler in me always stays busy. So, what did I decide to do in what was supposed to be my reflective period? I started an MBA program at five months pregnant. From the outside looking in, I know it sounds crazy and even a little overboard. What I learned is I was displacing all nervous energy and the yearning to hustle through pregnancy that I was losing sight of the beauty of what God had provided: the beauty of conceiving, despite questioning if I could have children, the beauty of God blessing me with a man who loves me unconditionally through my "isms" and my grind, and the beauty of a village who stood behind me to ensure I felt supported through this new journey. It was as if I was in a dream, and I questioned daily if I would wake up and all of it would disappear. So, I continued to go through the motions.

I was still traveling often for work, traveling to support friends, working all my businesses and then the addition of school. Items were being checked off the list, but there was no sense of balance or direction. I was going through the motions because I had committed to all these things, but my priorities were all over the place. I was not taking time to invest in self-care, not taking the time to allow God to bring balance, and not finding a sense of happiness. I was having the prenatal mommy blues, hustling to work through the pregnancy so my baby was set financially, and not adjusting any time to take breaks or to just breathe.

It was in the middle of my second trimester when God asked me to reflect on my spirituality, my emotions and my physical integrity, that I learned the why behind it. I woke up one morning with body aches, a bloody nose and sinus-like symptoms. After obtaining the services of "Doctor Google" to understand what was going on with me, I came to the conclusion that I may have COVID.

After taking the test and receiving the positive results, my mind was racing. How would COVID impact my pregnancy? How long will I have these symptoms? Is my unborn child feeling the sickness, the stress, and the emotions that I was putting out? It was in these moments where I realized, the "Hustler Lexx" and the way she operates no longer matters. If my child is impacted or our lives are impacted negatively because of my ways of continuing to travel everywhere, working long hours, running a business, running a non-profit and now back in school, I would be devastated. I knew change was a must! In the past, I went through periods where God slowed me down. But, I always ramped everything back up with work and hustle without a question. This time was different. This time was personal. This was beyond me and all the selfish ways had to go away.

A few weeks after recovering from COVID, Denzel and I went to our normal monthly check-up at 27 weeks pregnant. During this appointment, I had to get my blood drawn and the physician was measuring the length and weight of the baby. We learned that the growth of the baby was beginning to fall off the growth curve.

That day, I was categorized as "complicated pregnancy due to COVID-19 in the second trimester". Unfortunately, with COVID being so fresh, there were no answers. The physicians could not provide any medications without significant side effects, home remedies were not an option, and all other "solutions" were not supported by the data of pregnant woman with my genetic makeup. There was no significant sample of tests regarding my situation, because the world was still learning about COVID. My world felt like it was crashing. With all of the emotions going on and also trying not to put stress on my beautiful baby boy forming in my womb, how was I supposed to manage? Denzel and I, along with our families, relied on our foundation, the Lord and Savior, Jesus Christ. We were having many conversations with the Lord on our knees.

Our monthly appointments quickly changed from monthly to bi-weekly. These bi-weekly appointments consisted of fetal growth ultrasounds to monitor the baby closely and to continue to monitor my levels. At the next appointment, we learned that my platelet levels were also decreasing along with baby's growth. After researching for many hours, I thought I had a solution of what could be happening. My thoughts were that I was experiencing Hemodialysis Elevated Liver Enzymes, Low Platelets also known as HELLP syndrome. When Denzel and I brought this up to the physicians, it was hard for them to diagnose as they were still trying to understand how this all connects to COVID. A few weeks went by of us having bi-weekly appointments and one of my care physicians sat me down to provide a realistic picture of what was going on.

To give you a better picture of the scenario, I was sat down by a black physician for the first time in my pregnancy journey. She looked like me, delivered children of other black mothers through the pandemic, and took the time to read my chart and understand my lifestyle and what was going on. I began asking questions about the possibility of being induced and expressed my feelings that it was unnecessary. I let the doctor know how nervous I was, and how I had an entire birthing plan of an unmedicated, natural, vaginal birth. She patiently looked at me and listened. Then, she told me to sit back and get ready Christian, young lady and planner, "With a lot of unanswered questions in the world of maternity health as it relates to COVID, would you rather fight the induction?" She explained that other doctors would be coming around to pretty much try to experiment with me like a guinea pig of what could possibly be going on. She basically made it clear that induction was the safest route for me during the pandemic.

The questions were hitting me hard because there I was once again going through the motions and trying to be inspector gadget when the true mystery that I wanted to solve is for God to allow me to deliver my baby boy the healthiest way possible. After having this come to Jesus moment, I took all of the energy I was giving to work, friends, travel, and businesses and put it all on ice. All my energy from that point on would be centered around my baby's health and to the advocacy of my body. I had to take back control of what was going on with my health and the health of the baby.

One night, I stayed up and wrote a ten-page PowerPoint presentation on my wants and needs of my birth plan. It went into detail on how I wanted my spiritual, emotional and physical experience to be in my birthing room. I had to turn my hustle into mommy bear, mommy love and mommy protection mode. Every physician who I encountered from week 33 to week 39, I handed them a copy of the birth plan. I needed the hospital facility to know that although in my first trimester I was focused and distracted on all the wrong things, I was not an experiment. Although I was considered high-risk, my baby was my number one priority, and everyone was going to know God was the one who was going to deliver my baby boy into this world.

It was at 39 weeks that I was scheduled to go in for an induction. Of course, physicians were reminding me of my low platelet count, that it was unknown if my placenta was failing to provide nutrients to the baby, and so many additional scenarios. I got on my knees one last time and whispered, "Dear Lord, I am a victorious woman who you have blessed to conceive a child. I may have missed the signs that you wanted to me to sit down and truly enjoy the beauty of my pregnancy journey, but I'm present now. Every bit of pain, emotional toll and questions on why an unmedicated vaginal natural birth will only be answered by you".

On July 28, 2022, at 8:00 pm EST, I was admitted into the hospital to begin the induction. I asked my nursing staff to read over my birth plan once more and asked to not be questioned on COVID-19 or my decision to want a natural birth without medication. With God's hand directing my heart and emotions, and with the help of my amazing birthing team which consisted of my fiancé (Denzel), my mother and my mother-in-law to be, I gave birth to Daeton Amir Keyes at 2:09 pm EST…and it was an unmedicated, vaginal birth.

Sharing my story and journey to having my handsome, strong and healthy baby boy, Daeton, was not meant to scare new mommies or women who are considering being mommies. My story and testimony is being shared to provide a different outlook of seeing the red flags and finding true balance while on the journey to motherhood. As you are planning for your beautiful families, please do me a huge favor and DANCE:

D- Dedicate planned time for self-care

A- Awareness of activities or commitments which brings stress or greats amounts of work

N- Nurture your journey to motherhood and be vocal

C- Claim balance and peace

E- Enjoy motherhood and all its Glory

As you find time to DANCE, don't think you have to do it alone. Finding moms who know what you are going through and building a community is important. Talking to your elders on their experiences and having healthy dialogue on how their journey may differ from yours is healthy. Using your voice and saying 'no' to work, saying 'no' to side businesses and whatever else that may be distracting you from enjoying your journey to motherhood has to be controlled early on. Most importantly, find that Scripture, affirmation or encouraging phrase that will help get you through the tough days. Balance is not mastering it all at once, it is embracing that it evolves, and it is unique to you and your story.

P.S. Finding balance is ongoing! As God has used me to form a schedule and direction with my baby boy, God has now blessed me with a second baby on the way! Let's DANCE together ladies!

Blessings to all of the hustling mommies and mommies-to-be. I am rooting for you!

Chapter 3

Surrendering to the Process
Morgan Taylor-McFadden

---

*Surrender: to yield to the power, control, or possession
of another upon compulsion or demand.*

I remember I had this uncontrollable urge to organize and clean
my house the last few weeks leading up to my due date. I
wanted my environment to look, feel, and smell a certain way. It
was a bit compulsive, but I just knew that this is how I needed it
to be. Everyone, including my husband and six-year-old, had to
fall in line, or else. Everything needed to be in its proper place, the
pillows upright on the couch, the sink clear of dishes, and the
constant aroma of lavender and rose flowing through the rooms.
I guess you could say I was nesting, but in retrospect, I think it
was more than that.

I needed to be in control of something. After all, I was growing
a human in my body, and change was happening rapidly. My belly
was huge, my appetite was unfamiliar, my energy level was low
and my patience was thin. No, I had not an ounce of patience. I
couldn't participate in many activities I previously enjoyed, and
even if I wanted to, I had my family advising me on what I could
and couldn't do to keep the baby safe. It felt like everything was

centered around the baby. The first thing anyone would say to me was about the baby. "Oh, wow! You're so big, when are you due?" or "Pregnancy looks so good on you!" While I know folks meant no harm, it was these types of greetings that sometimes left me feeling insignificant. It felt like my identity was lost in the baby. I began to ask myself questions like, who am I, who am I becoming, and will I be enough? I felt as if I was losing myself. In fact, with this being my second child, it seemed as if my individuality was fleeting even further away. Internally, I was feeling like I was becoming invisible. Not only on the outside but on the inside, too. This was why those harmless greetings felt so triggering. I was struggling to just be.

Don't get me wrong, I was thrilled to be expecting my second daughter. Unlike my first pregnancy, this one was planned, and while I felt happy, I couldn't shake the underlying anxiety and sense of being out of control. As a woman of this generation, I believe it's almost ingrained to strive for control in life. We're conditioned to believe that hard work brings rewards, whether it's in relationships, salary, title, having a home, or simply feeling accomplished. The idea of success is ever-present, and we constantly feel the pressure to check off these boxes to achieve the life we desire. The fear of anything threatening this idea can send everything spiraling out of control.

Even with the awareness that life has more to offer than mere ambition, I've realized that maintaining balance requires an extraordinary amount of psychological reframing. It means not seeing setbacks as failures, but as opportunities to learn and grow. Additionally, incorporating regular yoga sessions into my routine has become essential to finding inner peace and reducing stress. These practices have become my lifeline, helping me navigate the demands of modern life and societal pressures. However, I must admit that sometimes, utilizing these tools can feel like a distant dream, especially during overwhelming circumstances.

Not many people talk about the unraveling or undoing that takes place during pregnancy. I would describe it as a beautiful nightmare that most people probably feel uncomfortable discussing. This doesn't mean you're not excited about the arrival of your new baby, or that you're not grateful for the miraculous ability to be a portal for life, it's just complicated. It's these complexities that make us human. Our greatest attributes are often at the root of what makes us who we are and is what makes us special.

A few weeks before my due date, my mom and niece flew into Boston from Los Angeles. It was the first time seeing my family during my pregnancy. Part of the reason for not connecting was the COVID-19 Pandemic. The other reason was obviously because of the distance. Seeing my family caused me to be so full of emotions. I was grateful to be able to finally spend some significant time with the people who meant so much to me.

Due to COVID being at its peak, giving birth in a hospital was the least bit appealing. The mere fact that I was a Black woman giving birth, meant I had to take certain precautionary measures to make sure that the standard of care I received was at a level I deserved and was entitled to. It didn't help that I was hyper-aware that Black women and babies have far less better birth outcomes. So, it made me go above and beyond to try and create the best birth plan I possibly could.

Our OB/GYN was not only one of the best in the area but also a Black woman, which brought me immense comfort given my anxieties. Additionally, we made the decision to hire a certified home-birth Midwife because we truly wanted to receive prenatal care and welcome our baby into the world in the familiar and secure surroundings of our home. To add to our good fortune, my niece graciously volunteered to be our doula. Given my own experience as a doula, I knew how crucial it was to have her by my side during the birth, offering valuable support in managing the emotional and physical demands that come with a home- birth experience. Quite plainly, it felt like we had it all figured out. Oh boy, was I wrong. Absolutely nothing went as we had planned.

I developed an immense amount of anxiety, which was opposite of my first pregnancy. With Isis, my greatest fear was considering the amount of pain I would feel. This time it was no longer the pain I was fearing, it was death. Although I was healthy and hopeful, honestly, I was scared I might not survive childbirth. My fear and understanding that I was a part of a system that often doesn't value the safety and thriving of people who look like me, had me constantly thinking about how I could prepare myself to make sure both Assata and I would make it out of this situation alive and well. Here I was, planning and trying my best to dictate outcomes based on my desire to survive. Don't get me wrong, there is a level of preparation and planning that is critical for anything you do, particularly in childbirth. Bringing a baby into the world is a huge deal that requires many considerations of the process both during and after.

I would have liked to have been more present. I realized later that I had spent so much time and energy trying to accomplish this ideal birthing experience, I didn't have much capacity to be fully present in my body to enjoy and embrace the fullness of being pregnant. I was always in the future, trying to control outcomes, thinking about the next phase, rather than being present in each moment. It was somewhat obsessive, and kind of like how I was with requiring order in my house. It had to be a certain way.

Assata was due on October 20th of 2020. This date had become cemented in my mind. Everything was planned around this date. I just knew she was going to either come a few weeks before, or on her due date at the latest. As I reflect, it's quite humorous that I thought for a second, she would come on my terms. I cringe just thinking about it, of course I was just plain wrong. As a birth worker/doula myself, I knew good and well that babies come when they are ready. Due dates are just estimates. But still, in my mind I had rationalized her punctual arrival based on the fact that her sister, six years prior, came on her exact due date. And yes, maybe I was reaching a bit. However, there was also evidence supporting that subsequent babies are likely to arrive earlier and easier. So, I figured Assata would arrive no later than October 20, 2020. Here I was again, thinking I could control the situation.

Of course, my due date came and left, only leaving me frustrated and anxious. I was doing every natural induction method I could just to get "lil momma" out. I was bouncing on exercise balls, drinking nasty castor oil, walking long distances, and eating spicy food…pretty much everything! There was an additional level of urgency to get my labor going because my doula (my niece, Mecca) would be returning to Los Angeles on the 29th. I was trying so hard to get the baby to come before she had to leave.

Stressing and anxious, I reached out to my midwife explaining to her how exhausted I was from the inconsistent contractions, and how much I just wanted the baby to come. Nothing we tried worked. The 29th ended up coming and leaving with my doula, and I was frustrated and deeply disappointed. Yet, I was still holding on to my plan for this "ideal birth". Assata (my strong-willed baby) had her own plan for how and when she would enter the world.

After many tear-filled conversations with my midwife, we decided that she would reach out to my OB to try and come up with another induction plan. Unconventional and outside of the scope of "natural", I was scheduled to take two doses of a cervical ripening pill at the hospital. The plan was that I would return home to hopefully fulfill my desired wish for an at-home water birth. Finally, a plan that gave me back some hope after being discouraged and flustered with the fact that my original plan was going to shit. I packed my bag, and my husband took me to the hospital for the first dose. When I arrived, the hospital staff took me back to the room, hooked me up to the heart and fetal monitors, and eventually gave me the pill.

While waiting, a nurse rushed into the room, started doing some assessments, asking questions, and then the OB on rounds came to tell me that I was going to have to be admitted. I was told the baby's heart rate dropped, and anytime that happens, admission is mandatory. They said it was likely that her hand may have just pushed down on the umbilical cord. But regardless, it was their standard protocol to admit when that occurs.

At that point, my defenses began to fall. I called my mom and husband to let them know what was happening. I told them that they needed to prepare to come to the hospital because the delivery plan had now changed. I let them know that everything was fine, but due to Assata's heart rate dropping the hospital requires mandatory admission. You can imagine that I was heartbroken. The beautiful home birth that I envisioned was for sure not going to happen. I sat with grief for a little while and cried. I allowed my tears to flow, and remembered thinking that the most important outcome from all of this was the two of us making it out alive. Our safety and livelihood were more valuable than the experience and money spent trying to create the home-birthing experience we so badly hoped for. I finally arrived at a place of surrender. Although it took some time to get here, I was feeling freer, and this was the beginning of the turning point.

My husband and mother arrived a few hours later with my repacked hospital bag, that now accounted for the additional days the baby and I would be expected to stay. My six-year old was situated with family members, and we all exhaled and embraced the new reality. We would not be in a pool in my guest room. We would be in a bed, in a hospital room. Settling more into surrender, my focus dialed back, and my attention was now centered around only my breath and the little life that was inside of me preparing to make her debut.

Breathing through each of my contractions, my labor began to progress. Little by little, I released the need to try and control my external environment. I was relinquishing my expectations which in turn created space for me to solely focus on getting this baby here safely.

The pain grew more intense by the hour. I was extremely uncomfortable. I thought I had lost my doula when my niece had to return to Los Angeles. Thankfully, I had the support of my husband and mother who found ways to help manage my pain through it all. They played music, kept me hydrated, and rubbed me down until I fell asleep. I so strongly resisted a hospital birth, but it ended up persisting in the long run. It wasn't what I wanted, but I was grateful that I had support and a care team that saw me as human and responded to my every need. I didn't know then, but I was slowly redefining my definition of an ideal birth.

I remember the anesthesiologist came to the room a second time to talk about pain management options. I had already declined the epidural earlier because, at the time, I was still holding on to this idea of a "natural birth". I wanted a home birth, a water birth, no medication, no hospital, all natural! I was so stuck on this fallacy that I was ignoring the truth. I remember so clearly, after having already endured over 24 hours of heavily painful contractions, my mom saying, "Morgan, you don't have to be in this much pain. It is okay to get an epidural. Why are you putting yourself through this? (pain) What are you trying to prove, and to whom?" That's when it hit me! I fully surrendered at that point. I really let it all go. I let go of the control, the expectations, the fight against systemic medical racism, the false perceptions, and my rigid success plan. There were many good reasons why I built these barriers, and there was evidence to support why I established these conditions. But, I wasn't assessing the truth in my circumstances. I lacked flexibility, and inadvertently my own self-judgment was creating a more toxic birth environment. Regardless of any intervention you consent to, there is nothing more natural than childbirth.

I surrendered completely to the power of birth, allowing my body to do what it was created to do. Surrender took on a new meaning. It meant surrendering to the sleepless nights and the constant demands of motherhood. It meant surrendering to the uncertainty and the messiness of raising a child. It meant surrendering to the inevitable changes that come with welcoming a new life into the world. Through it all, I've learned that surrender is not a sign of weakness but a profound act of strength. It is the acknowledgment that there are forces greater than us at play, and that sometimes the best thing we can do is let go and trust the process. Surrendering allowed me to embrace the fullness of my experience as a woman, a mother, and a person.

So, while pregnancy may have initially sparked a desire for control within me, it ultimately led me on a journey of surrender—a journey that continues to unfold as I navigate the beautiful chaos of motherhood. And in the surrender, I have found a profound sense of liberation, self-discovery, and an unwavering connection to the incredible power of the human body and spirit.

After returning home with my new baby, it took me several months to fully reflect on my entire birth experience. Although there were still lingering traces of grief over not having a home-birth, I managed to work through those feelings. I now had a healthy baby, adding to my already beautiful family of four, and I myself was on the path to recovery with the support I received. This entire process taught me valuable lessons about life. It reminded me that not every situation unfolds as we envision, yet there can still be moments of joy along the way. Life is filled with unpredictable ups and downs, much like the journey of birth. Assata, in her own way, taught me the importance of surrender. I realized that letting go can bring abundance beyond what we cling to. I discovered that I gained so much more than what I initially believed I had lost. I also learned the significance of preparing and being aware when entering situations like birth. It's crucial to be adaptable and fully present, embracing the process, practicing patience, nurturing oneself, and accepting support. By tuning into the present moment, listening to our bodies becomes easier. Trusting our instincts and acknowledging that we already possess everything we need are key elements to remember.

Additionally, here are some practical tips that can help you to navigate and surrender to birth's unexpected and expected challenges.

Embrace the Unexpected: Birth is full of surprises, and sometimes things don't go as planned. Embrace the unpredictability and find joy in the journey, even when the outcome isn't what you envisioned.

Practice Surrender: Learn the art of surrendering to circumstances beyond your control. Letting go of expectations and attachments can open doors to new possibilities and bring unexpected abundance into your life. Most of the time, it's going to end up okay!

Find Value in Loss: When faced with loss or disappointment, remember that there is often more to gain than what you may initially perceive. Look for the hidden lessons, growth, and opportunities that can arise from challenging experiences.

Prepare and Stay Present: Prioritize preparation and awareness when entering important situations. Whether it's birth or any other significant event, do your due diligence, plan accordingly, and stay flexible in the face of changing circumstances. Being fully present allows you to navigate challenges with greater ease.

Seek Support and Cultivate Patience: Surround yourself with a supportive network of loved ones who can assist you during difficult times. Practice patience with yourself and the process, understanding that healing and growth take time.

Listen to Your Body: Tune in to your body's signals and cues. Trust your instincts and intuition, as they often guide you toward what you truly need. Prioritize self-care and well-being, as it directly impacts your ability to navigate difficult moments.

Embrace the Present Moment: Embracing the present moment allows you to fully experience life and make the most of every situation. Let go of worries about the past or future and focus on what is happening right now with you. This mindset enables you to appreciate the journey and find peace amidst uncertainty.

Believe in Yourself: Remind yourself that you possess everything you need within you. Trust in your own capabilities, strengths, and intuition. Cultivate self-belief and confidence, knowing that you are capable of navigating through ups and downs.

Remember, these tips are inspired by personal experiences, and applying them to your own life may require adaptation based on your unique circumstances. But most of all…you got this, Sis!

Chapter 4

Body Image

Nigerain Collier

When my husband and I found out I was pregnant we were both more than excited. I was looking forward to the baby bump and the glowing skin that you hear so much about. With my anxiety at an all-time high and my heart beating through my chest, I was ready and somewhat scared of all the changes that were to come. We already started the race, so I was looking forward to the journey and ready for the finish line (or at least I thought).

When it comes to pregnancy, oftentimes you hear all the glorious stories (some of them horror stories), but what about the physical changes that no one talks about? You know what I mean. Yes, you expect a huge belly, stretch marks and now you have boobs that are bigger than you imagined. But, what about the things that you didn't expect? My body has always been my body. Then, I woke up one day sharing it with someone I didn't even know. If you're expecting, you'll probably experience being overwhelmed with emotions. Trust me, you are not alone. A wave of thoughts came running through my head: will I "snap back", how big will I get, and does everyone's nose actually spread? These were just some of the things that were racing through my head. I know it sounds scary but stick with me it gets better I promise.

Accepting all these changes was a process, but it was one that I knew would pay off in the end. My body wasn't the only thing that was changing. I felt as though I had so many people telling me things about myself and what I should and shouldn't do. I don't know how many times I heard "you are the type of person that is going to "snap" right back, make sure you're putting lotion on your stomach every day, and don't forget to walk so your healing process is smoother". I was so scared of what my new body would look like and how I would feel in it.

Let me take you on a journey with me before my body was invaded by a little person. I promise I won't scare you. It all comes full circle in the end. Before the announcement of my beautiful baby girl my body was "snatched". I didn't have hips and dips. However, I did have a slim waist, defined abs, and legs for days. I'm sure we can all agree that we have parts of ourselves that we wouldn't mind improving. But, I learned to love the skin I was in. Flaws and all, it was my body. My fashion sense was always a form of expression for me. I wore what I liked, and I wore what felt good. Shopping had always been a hobby of mine, and it was always easy for me to find my size. Believe it or not I've pretty much always been the same weight my whole life with minor changes of course. After finding out I was pregnant, I knew my style would have to change. Don't get me wrong, Mama, you can still be a fashionista. However, you'll find that pregnancy is all about being as comfortable as possible. Changes were on their way, and I could see them day by day; sometimes it felt like overnight. I can recall everyday looking in the mirror, turning side-to-side to see if my baby bump was growing. My husband brought up the idea of us documenting the entire pregnancy, and that's what we did. From the second we left the hospital to confirm we were pregnant, I started holding my stomach with a smile on my face and a camera recording. The baby was the size of a grain of rice, and I was already rubbing my belly. Every week was a new picture and a new update on my beautiful round bump. The first couple of weeks, I noticed I was growing pretty fast. Remember, I told you I had always been small. So, any changes my body made were easily noticeable. It was exciting to look back on pictures over the weeks and see how I was transitioning into my new mom body. My boobs were filling out, my stomach was growing, and I had a booty. These changes were exciting, but quite different for me.

It was as though I was being pulled into two different directions, on one hand I absolutely loved my growing baby bump, my smooth skin, and my little waddle. On the other hand, I was missing my small waist and slim figure. There was guilt of not initially being over the moon about my pregnant body. I felt as though saying it out loud would make me seem ungrateful.

People started telling me that they could see changes in my face, and that the pregnancy was starting to show. That was scary for me. I know they meant no harm by their comments. They were just showing excitement about my pregnancy, but my body dysmorphia was real. I didn't know if it would just happen for me.

My aunts were consistently telling me every chance they got that I needed to oil up my stomach as much as possible to avoid stretch marks. Every phone call would somehow end up with them asking if I was well moisturized. To be honest, no. I wasn't focused on having stretch marks so I didn't feel like every second of the day I needed to be greased up like a turkey on Thanksgiving. Out of all the things that I was scared of, the idea of stretch marks wasn't one of them.

Don't get me wrong I did use Bio-Oil as a part of my nightly routine. However, it was not in my hourly routine. Stretch marks were like battle scars to me. They were going to show the hard work my body put in, and I was going to have curves. The women I knew who had stretch marks also had curves. So, I was looking forward to becoming a member of the "curvy" club. So, put it on my tab and welcome me to the party. I didn't have one stretch mark until about two weeks before my delivery. It was as if my body was playing a game of peek a boo to see if I was paying attention. I can vividly remember looking in the mirror at my baby bump (as we do so much around this time). I turned to the right and BOOM! It was as if overnight a group of long dark marks decided to stretch up the side of my stomach. I'm guessing my belly was too smooth and needed a little "razzle dazzle" for dramatic effect. I noticed that after birth more appeared out of the nowhere, and some in places that I didn't think to check. A lot of times you will hear people say that they are permanent which can be scary in the grand scheme of things, because most pregnancy symptoms do go away after birth. However, once again you are different and uniquely made, Mama. Your marks can lighten up, fade, or even become so unnoticeable it's as if they were never there to begin with. Your stretch marks are like tiger stripes, no one stripe is the same and no one pregnancy journey is the exact same either. Enjoy it all for its underlined beauty. Social media isn't reality. But, your process and how you handle it is.

As I watched my body growing, I didn't know if I would be one of the lucky ones who just "snapped" back. Subconsciously, I had this pressure of making sure that I maintained my physical image after birth. What's even worse is that I had no idea as to how I was going to maintain my physique after birth. Do I work out? Do I diet? I was beginning to love the new body I was in and at the same time miss the body I once had. I tried my hardest to ignore my feelings of mourning and guilt. But honestly, it was hard. I knew that pregnancy was a blessing and that it was beautiful. However, some changes came as a complete surprise, and I felt caught off guard.

I've heard uncomfortable stories and seen videos on social media of women whose skin broke out a little or they got a shade or two darker than before. But, have you ever had hyperpigmentation going straight down your legs and back acne? Now this is not one of those stories about your baby ruining your body and you never being the same. This is me being honest with you and telling you that your body is wonderfully made, and some changes are going to be unique just like the beautiful child you're carrying.

I had a unique form of hyperpigmentation, something I had never heard of before. I'll never forget asking my doctor if the discoloration on my legs were normal. I had a line so dark separating each leg. You would've thought I was a Dalmatian. I vividly remember him responding, "In all my years I have never seen that before?" Here I am sitting on the doctor's table thinking, "well, you are supposed to have all the answers". I followed up by asking him if it would go away? These changes had to be because of the baby, right? Didn't that mean that after the baby was here my body would go back to normal? Right?! Boy, was I wrong. To be honest, you won't be the same mentally, physically, or emotionally, and some of those unique changes won't go away. Instead, they will uniquely be a part of your own personal journey to motherhood. You are perfectly made. Changes and all, you will be just the way you were intended to be. This process is beautiful, it's personal, and there's always something new. No day is like the one before. That's boring, and that typically is not how motherhood goes.

A lot of times social media was a battle on its own for me. It was as if my social media algorithm knew that I was expecting. Every post was of a new mom breastfeeding, someone who just went into labor, or a mom showing off how she "snapped" back in a month. To make matters worse, it was as if everyone I knew was pregnant, too. I couldn't help but to compare. Everywhere I looked, women were glowing and living their best life while I am at home trying not to throw up every chance I get. Oh, and let's not forget this mom who is drinking a healthy smoothie every morning. Meanwhile, I can't help but want my cravings for french fries and ketchup. I'm scrolling down my timeline, I'm seeing moms further along than me working out and eating healthy. They had me questioning if I was doing enough… "am doing pregnancy right?" Even after birth, I was trying to figure out why my body didn't magically "snap" back like the girl on my timeline.

Here I am two months postpartum and my body looks like hers when she was one week postpartum.

As nasty as comparisons can be, you are human. When you are pregnant, and even after pregnancy, it is hard not to compare yourself. We tend to compare ourselves to our moms, our aunties, and even our friends when it comes to our pregnancy experience. Social media is no different but remember that you are. Remember, you are different and so is your body, your time and your experience. This is your time regardless of who is in a similar spot as you. As much as social media might cause you to question your journey and compare yourself, always remember that no one is like you. The same way that you notice someone else and their process, trust me, someone is comparing themselves to you.

The truth of the matter is, no matter if it is a planned pregnancy or a surprise, some things are to be expected and others are not. You typically hear that after six weeks postpartum you are clear to work out and do other extracurricular activities. Unfortunately, that was not the case for me, I was looking forward to starting my postpartum fitness journey but my body had other plans. I went in for my postpartum six week appointment eager to ask my doctor all my prepared questions, one of which was being cleared to work out. It was to my surprise that his answer was 'no'. I was not cleared to do certain exercises because I had an umbilical hernia due to pushing and diastasis recti (a big word to say abdominal separation). Honestly, I was sad and a little confused. It was my first time being pregnant let alone having a baby so it took me a few tries to get the pushing thing down, so the hernia made sense. However, the hernia left a bulge in my stomach that protrudes outwards which looks like I have a gut. Sadly, there is nothing I could do about it especially if I was considering having another child one day. If we wanted to work on baby number two, it was a possibility that I could get a hernia again. So, getting it surgically removed was pointless.

When I was pregnant, I would bend over to pick things up instead of squatting. So, learn from me, and make sure you bend with your knees and squat to lift anything. Better yet, don't lift anything heavy at all. The bending over topped with the weight of the baby, and the changes my body was going through, caused my muscles to separate. My muscles were kind of like an upside down peace sign. It didn't mean I could never workout out again. It just meant that I had to do certain exercises to cater to my condition. Yes, I wanted abs again but I didn't want to make it worse by doing crunches. Instead, I had to do oblique workouts to strengthen that muscle and push them back together. Other than my husband, I hadn't told anyone about what was going on with my body. So, imagine how I felt when the unsolicited opinions came rolling in. I had people close to me asking me when I was going to start working out to lose my stomach. To make matters worse, they would remind me of how small I was and would say things like "you don't want to have a gut", "I liked how small you were before", "don't let yourself go", "when your husband met you you were small". This was so upsetting to hear, because I knew for a fact that my husband loved me exactly the way I was. My husband appreciates me so much because he saw everything I had to go through to bring our child into this world.

These people had no idea that I was dealing with something that weights and a gym couldn't fix.

I was already trying to accept the fact that I would have to handle my recovery differently because of the diastasis recti. So, the opinions of others was the last thing that I needed. I was overwhelmed by the responses and tried to focus on working on my body. I knew I couldn't continue to listen to the comments and had to create boundaries for myself and unsolicited comments about my body.

You should always know your limits on how much you can take, and what you are and aren't okay with. Looking back, I realize I should have had certain boundaries in place before the pregnancy. But, the pregnancy ended up highlighting the importance of this for me, and I hope you understand the necessity of boundaries, also.

You should never allow anyone to speak negatively about your body regardless of the tone or meaning behind it. I understand all too well being strong and letting some things roll off. But, you have to have limits and be able to voice those limits to others. Going through something you're not comfortable sharing with others makes it even more important to speak up for yourself and draw those lines in the sand. You don't ever have to overshare, and you never have to tolerate someone making you feel bad about you.

Although I knew the people in my life meant no harm by commenting on my appearance, some things I wasn't okay hearing because of what I was dealing with in silence. Typically, we're already our own worst critics. So, the last thing we need is hearing unpleasant things on top of what we already say to ourselves. Speak up!

You have the right to say you don't like people touching your belly, or that you don't want anyone kissing or touching your baby's face. Love yourself and your body, Mama! Body image and beauty tend to have unrealistic standards, and it's not your job to try to live up to anyone else's standards and perceptions of you. The only person you have to impress is the reflection staring back at you.

I had to remind myself that my body went through a variety of changes throughout pregnancy and after. My path was the growing baby bump, hyperpigmentation, and unsolicited advice. It took my body nine months to create all these changes, and I had to finally come to terms with the fact that in my case, it may take that same amount of time for it to naturally take its new form.

Well, you've read and got a glimpse of the most vulnerable parts of my experience with pregnancy. Now, I want to speak life into you: (1) Give yourself grace, (2) give yourself time and (3) understand that your body is unique. Your body is powerful, strong and made especially for this. Whether this is your first pregnancy or your third, this is a chance for you to acknowledge and appreciate all the wonderful things that your body can do. Every child is different, every labor is different, and everybody is uniquely made. There will be changes you're not too comfortable with, and that's okay. There will also be moments that catch you by surprise. But, you have to remember that you are perfectly made.

Changes and all, you will be just the way you were intended to be. This process is beautiful, it's yours, and you should expect that there will always be something new. No day is like the one before. That would be boring, and definitely not how motherhood goes. So, consider this your head start. Learn to appreciate the experience. If you feel guilty about not enjoying the wave of changes your body is going through, remember you are not alone.

You created a living, breathing human and that is powerful. Your baby will forever be a reminder that it was all worth it. Throughout your life you have had many changes, physically, mentally and emotionally. This is no different. Yes, these physical changes come a lot quicker than most. Rest assured, you are so much stronger than you know. Accepting all of these differences can feel like a lot of pressure. But don't forget, pressure makes diamonds and that's what you are. labor is different, and everybody is uniquely made. There will be changes you're not too comfortable with, and that's okay. There will also be moments that catch you by surprise. But, you have to remember that you are perfectly made.

Changes and all, you will be just the way you were intended to be. This process is beautiful, it's yours, and you should expect that there will always be something new. No day is like the one before. That would be boring, and definitely not how motherhood goes. So, consider this your head start. Learn to appreciate the experience. If you feel guilty about not enjoying the wave of changes your body is going through, remember you are not alone.

You created a living, breathing human and that is powerful. Your baby will forever be a reminder that it was all worth it.

Throughout your life you have had many changes, physically, mentally and emotionally. This is no different. Yes, these physical changes come a lot quicker than most. Rest assured, you are so much stronger than you know. Accepting all of these differences can feel like a lot of pressure. But don't forget, pressure makes diamonds and that's what you are.

Chapter 5

Mom Guilt

Dynika Marshall

Mommies, do you sometimes find yourself having a feeling of guilt when it comes to your littles ones? It can often be perceived as a tiny voice inside or in the back of your mind instructing you that you are not good enough, you are not worthy enough, or you are not fit enough. This feeling of guilt mommies experience in relation to their child or children is called "mom guilt". This feeling can intensely arise in new mommies the most, but all mommies are susceptible to "mom guilt" at some stage during their motherhood journey. To be clear, guilt has the potential to extend to any parent of the child or any guardian of the child, but mothers are often the ones that society holds to a higher standard. Therefore, the feeling of guilt is commonly felt in mothers.

For example, have you ever dealt with having to choose between giving attention to your newborn baby and giving attention to your job? Have you ever dealt with having to choose your needs before your child's need at any specific moment? Have you had to make the decision of breastfeeding your child or having to feed your child formula? Have you ever felt too tired to play with your child? Have you ever lost your temper with your child? All those examples can lead to some form of "mom guilt". You will feel guilty about some choices you will have to make along the way. We as mommies constantly worry about failing or making mistakes and trying to get everything right on this motherhood journey. "Mom guilt" occurs from an unrealistic ideal of what a perfect mother should be, but it is important to identify and remember we are not alone in feeling this way. However, we most certainly do not have to adapt to or accept the feelings of "mom guilt".

So, let me take you through my motherhood journey of how I dealt with "mom guilt", ways that I was able to overcome it, and even ways that I am continuing to overcome as I am faced with new challenges every day.

I became a mother and a "mom girl" back in May 2021. So, my pregnancy was during the peaks of COVID, and as you can imagine it was not my ideal pregnancy process. I always thought that my pregnancy journey would be filled with many family members by my side, many nesting moments with my girls, my husband being able to join me at the doctor visits, me delivering my baby and my mom standing right by my side to help me welcome my baby into the world. But, my ideal pregnancy process was not my experience. Faced with reality and being pregnant during the COVID season, I was not able to share my most precious moments with my spouse, close family members, nor friends. I was not able to share that moment when I heard my child's first heartbeat with my husband. My husband was not able to hold my hand during the many doctor visits nor see our sweet baby girl on the sonogram screen. I was not allowed to have family members by my side as we awaited the delivery of my baby. Even during post-delivery, it was hard for family members to welcome our newborn home. It was just nerve-racking that we could potentially be exposed to COVID, and with a newborn we wanted to eliminate all exposure where possible. All these experiences made me feel alone and somewhat disconnected, which turned into a form of guilt for me. Not understanding that it was a form of guilt at the time, but it settled in as an uneasy feeling throughout my pregnancy/delivery journey.

I recall the exact day when my doctor and I made the decision to have a cesarean delivery for my child. At the time, it was one of the hardest moments in my life for me to accept and stick with that decision. I was about seven months or so and I had just had a sonogram screening performed. The doctor came in and told me that my child had grown at an enormous rate. I asked her to explain, because I did not quite understand. Month after month, going from my first trimester to my second trimester, my daughter seemed to be growing at an enormous rate. This raised concerns for the doctor, which led to the decision to have a cesarean delivery. The doctor's concern was that if the baby was larger than normal (over nine pounds) there could be a factor that she could potentially get stuck during delivery. At any given cost they would get the baby out but that could potentially mean breaking bones to retrieve the baby, cutting me to get the baby, etc. Hearing all of that alarmed me and I instantly committed to the safest route possible for delivery, which led to the decision of a cesarean birth.

After making this decision I cried and cried and cried! I already felt less than a mother because I would have to have a cesarean delivery and would not deliver vaginally. For a considerable number of mothers, undergoing a cesarean delivery causes feelings of disappointment and shame. I will be one hundred percent transparent! I immediately felt disappointed, less than, and a failure of a mother because of the great emphasis put on natural vaginal births by popular culture and social media!

Dealing with the emotional stressors of post-delivery (post cesarean delivery), I had to learn that it was going to take time to heal emotionally. I had to recognize I could not put a time limit on how long it would take, and to give myself grace in knowing that I was taking all the right steps to healing emotionally. I had to understand, that in my position, I was making the healthiest choice for myself and my baby, and that was okay. I was absolutely acting as a mother should! The feelings of disappointment that I was not experiencing a natural vaginal birth gradually went away as I understood the fact that I experienced my own unique birthing experience that could not be replicated by anyone else.

As I got over the hump of "mom guilt", I did not realize there would be so many future moments to come that would create this exact same feeling. As I began to prepare to return to work after having my daughter, I began to feel a sense of anxiety. I begin to feel anxious with the preparation of getting back to work on time and getting back into the swing of things. Not to mention, that I would be returning to a new role (I was promoted to manager while on leave). I wanted to return to work better than ever and thrive within my new role, but I had no idea what that looked like and felt like having a newborn at home. I was accustomed to waking up getting myself ready, moving at my own pace, going about my day thinking only of myself, but life as I knew it had drastically changed.

Thankfully, my job provides one of the most beneficial maternity leave packages that there is in Corporate America, and that was such a blessing for me and my husband to have so much time off with our baby girl. Just to give you some context and background of my job, it is very fast-paced, intense when it comes to particular clients, and forever evolving. I tried to prepare myself as much as possible with timing, family schedules, family meals, etc., but there was no amount of preparation that could fully prepare me to enter the workplace again with a newborn. When I returned to work, I immediately started working a lot of hours. I worked so much that my husband would come in our home office (we worked remotely for part of the week) and remind me that I hadn't seen our daughter all day. I began to struggle with spending more time at work or doing my work than with spending time with our newborn and my husband. Work became an all around the clock thing for me because I wanted to prove to myself that I had earned my new role and that I was deserving. This put a lot of pressure on my husband to do more things around the house and be the first responder to our daughter due to his job not being as time sensitive. I began to feel less than again because I was not able to put more time in with our daughter and I felt my job took precedence at the time. I began to feel unhappy with myself and more stressed than usual.

The factors of my job were still the same but what changed was I had a new addition to my family that quickly shifted my reality. I had to realign and figure out what was important to me again. Once I did, I realized that spending time with my family, giving our daughter the attention she needs, being there for morning drop offs, walks in the park, and being present for other activities was important to me. I wanted to be present and active, which I knew would require me to shift some things in my work life! I learned how to set boundaries with work and focus separately on my family. I blocked out periods of time on my calendar for dropping off my daughter for daycare, walks in the neighborhood with my daughter, and preparing meals ahead of time. When I set those boundaries, there were no more work disruptions and I could be focused and present.

Work did not stop nor did the emails. So, once we were able to get our daughter into bed for the night, I would hop back online to continue working, close out what I could, and prepare for the next day. The difference now is I had a cut off time set so I wouldn't be working throughout the night. I would spend no more than an hour and a half finishing work for the day. As hard as it was to disconnect, it is absolutely necessary to keep the sanity between work and family life.

After getting somewhat of a handle on work and balancing my family life (it's a continued work in progress) I still had to find time for me, I had to find time to cater to my needs to refill my cup and replenish the energy that I needed for myself. I found it extremely challenging to proactively prioritize my self-care to the extent that I forgot who I was before having a child. I forgot how

I even prioritized myself prior to and what it even felt like to invest in myself, and when I did manage to find small windows and pieces of time for self-care, the "mom guilt" quickly set in immediately after! Over time, I had to learn that self-care was not selfish at all, it was in fact an essential part of me being a good wife and mother. Practicing self-care and doing the things that cater to my needs helped me to be a better mother. The more I started to give to myself the more I had to give to my daughter and my family. And this did not just happen overnight, I had to actually carve out time for myself and be consistent with the time that I scheduled. I set a particular time on a particular day so that my husband knew this was the time I was using for myself, and whatever I felt like on that day is what occupied my time. Whether that was taking a long bubble bath, going to the movies by myself, or taking myself out to eat, that scheduled time was for me to do whatever I needed to do in that moment to give back to myself.

Fast forward to present. It's Summer 2023, and I am an expecting mother again of another baby girl. Even this scenario can spike "mom guilt" at times. Being pregnant while raising a toddler is the complete opposite of my first pregnancy experience. During my first pregnancy I was able to rest and take naps when I needed to, I was able to cater to that self-care that I just spoke about, and I was still able to move around as an independent individual while preparing for the birth of my child. This time around the pregnancy looks and feels so much different. I have concerns about holding my daughter while being pregnant. I often wonder am I putting too much pressure on my unborn child, am I lifting too much, and am I neglecting my daughter if I do not pick her up when needed? In other moments when I am extremely tired (especially during my first trimester) and needed rest or I needed some time to myself and I chose to do that over spending time with my daughter, that often triggers a feeling of guilt for me. Being pregnant is tiring. Having a toddler is tiring. So, the combination of both happening simultaneously is extremely tiring. But, I am learning to conserve my energy whenever I can. My mother often comes to the house and volunteers to wash the dishes, vacuum the floor, or just does things to help around the house. Instead of me feeling as if she is criticizing me because my house is not together, I allow her to help to take some of the burden off me. This allows me to rest a bit and take some much-needed time. In addition to this, Im also finding ways that my toddler can help me throughout the pregnancy process. For instance, I encourage her to take certain things to the trash, I encourage her to climb into her car seat by herself, and I allow her to carry certain small groceries into the house after grocery shopping. This takes a load off me and allows her to be independent in her own way and so far, it is working so I am loving it.

With many known factors (some of which I touched on in this chapter but there are many others) that can trigger "mom guilt", we must find ways to deal with it and ultimately overcome it! We have to stay grounded in maternal wellness, which is all about prioritizing and finding room for yourself, so that we can enjoy the life of motherhood even with the challenges that it brings. Here are a few tips to take with you if you ever experience "mom guilt" along your motherhood journey!

Tip #1: Let go of / make peace with "mom guilt".

If "mom guilt" decides to show up at your door, practice actually working through the guilt by not being shocked or surprised when it shows up. Let go of others' expectations of what a mother looks like. We have to change our mindsets and reframe our thoughts on what it means to be a good mother. Take the pressure of society off because that is not reality! Identifying the source of guilt can also help us realize what areas in our lives we need to pay more attention to. Sometimes the source can be external or internal by preset expectations we received from others, or by the expectations we put on ourselves. When we work to identify what source matters the most to us, we can define our true values of what motherhood means to us.

Tip #2: Understand and lock in with your new reality.

Identify what will help you have a good day and what will help you have a good week. Once those identifiers have been confirmed you will be able to practice that in future weeks which will ultimately become routine and create the environment you want and can thrive in.

What does your sleep routine look like now? Do you have to go to sleep earlier? Do you have to go to sleep later? Whatever that perfect combination is, work towards that goal every night so you can develop good sleeping habits.

How do you make the most of your time now? How is your time managed? Setting constant routines throughout the day to help you make the most of your time will be extremely beneficial for you and your family. Maybe that looks like setting out clothes the night before, prepping food the night before, and getting everything prepped so you're ready to go in the mornings! That can help you out drastically!

Have you identified your stressors? Is your mental health impacted? If you are an absentee parent, your child will ultimately be affected causing them to have issues in their adult life.

Learning to identify your stress triggers can benefit you in a profound way. Plan ahead to help minimize your stress triggers as much as possible. Take your "me time" when needed to alleviate burnout. Pray and meditate to develop calming routines that create a stable mindset.

Tip #3: Remember your identity beyond motherhood and invest in yourself.

It is extremely easy to lose yourself when caring for your children. Women are nurturers, so our first instinct is to give, give, and give. We have to come to terms with taking the necessary quality time that we need for ourselves. Remember the things that made us curious, confident, sexy, and alive. Begin to act on those things and find time to make room for them. Invest time and energy in things that will refill you and benefit you in the long run such as workout sessions, a walk in the park, visiting art galleries, a night out with the girls or date night with your significant other. Remember that you are a role model for your children. So, prioritizing your care is just as important for them to see as it is for you to do!

If things become too burdensome always seek the help that you need because your little ones are depending on you. As I end this chapter, I leave you with you with my final thoughts:

Find the right balance that works for you.

Allow yourself grace on the journey of motherhood.

Acknowledge the smalls wins.

Consistently pour into you so that you are fueled.

Best wishes on your motherhood journey.

Chapter 6

Breastfeeding Journey
Rodneshia Seals

It is said that black women have the lowest breastfeeding rate and even if we do choose to breastfeed, we don't do it long term. I have a huge family and I didn't grow up knowing much about breastfeeding. My mom had an in-home daycare, and all the babies were on formula. I used to help her out, so I remember the formula being in an aluminum can, the same as canned veggies and fruits. I would open it with a can opener and mix it with water in a Kool-Aid jug. I was excited when it eventually went to ready-made bottles and eventually to powder form. That made it easier to transport. Anyone could feed a formula fed baby and the process just seemed easy. I would overhear all the women in my family speak about using cabbage leaves to dry up their milk. I never witnessed this process, but I am certain that it worked because year after year I would hear about it.

Breastfeeding just wasn't the first choice for whatever reason and they didn't have the time to dedicate to the process. I'm black. My relatives are black and the women who utilized my mom's in-home daycare were black. They had to work and at the time they had jobs, not careers. So, I can imagine how hard it would have been trying to pump and maintain the milk throughout the workday. As I stated before, anyone could help with feedings when the baby was on formula, and that included the younger siblings and relatives. For my family and probably many more, formula was the best option to fit their situation.

When I was a teenager, I witnessed someone "nursing" for the first time. It was at that moment that I decided that if I ever had a baby I didn't want to breastfeed because it looked "too intimidating" for my liking. I couldn't imagine my baby hanging on my breast. Nope! Didn't want it. Fast forward a few years, I'm walking around Walmart and there is a section that is empty with pieces of paper stating there was a formula shortage. I passed right by because that didn't pertain to me, or so I thought. About a month after that Walmart visit, I found out I was pregnant. By now, every woman close to me that had a baby, nursed. I had picked their brains about it and watched my cousin fill her fridge with milk to the point that she needed a deep freezer. She made it look so easy and helped change my mind about it. Even if I wanted to choose formula, I couldn't due to the shortage. So, I needed to nurse. I soaked up all the knowledge I could from those around me and read different articles up until it was time to have the baby. I was still nervous about the process, but I was ready. I was choosing to trust my body.

The day after delivery, there were so many people in and out of my room. One sweet lady came in my room with a small yellow and white pump with her and some bins. She introduced herself as my lactation consultant. She educated me on latching, colostrum, tongue ties, flange size and so much more. She showed me how to properly clean and dry pump parts in the bins. She taught me about let down phases and different pump settings. I was overwhelmed, but I knew breastfeeding didn't just mean I nursed the baby, pumping was included in this process as well. I remember thinking about my dog and cat and how they knew what to do without me educating them on anything and that kind of reassured me that I would be just fine. We also went over different ways to hold the baby while nursing and finally it was time to try. What my lactation consultant failed to mention was how isolating and lonely my journey was about to become. She didn't mention the uneasiness that would consume anyone in the same room as us if my baby needed to eat. She told me to drink water, but she didn't tell me that I would instantly feel the dryness in my mouth as he nursed, during feedings I could easily down a gallon of water. There was so much left unsaid that I would figure out on my own throughout my postpartum period.

When my son latched for the first time it was a little painful and honestly it caught me off guard. I didn't expect that little mouth to have such great suction. But, the moment I looked down and watched him eat I fell in love. My body was providing him with everything he needed. I needed this connection and this bond.

Once I was home and there was no lactation specialist ready to come in at the press of a button and that is when "shit got real." We ended up having to go get nipple shields because my baby was fussy and hungry, my nipples were too small, and he had a tongue tie that I didn't get cut in the hospital. The nipple shields were a God send. As soon as I would place it on, I could see my nipple swell up inside it and I knew my baby would be able to latch. We used the shield for about three weeks and then one day he just latched perfectly. Having to keep up with the shield or fumbling around with it at night was a nightmare. I was glad to throw those things out.

Around week two, I had my first run in with engorgement. It started in just one breast and eventually both were swollen and tight. I had a heating pad on them and tried to let the baby nurse to alleviate the pain, but it was too bad. I spoke with the wife of one of my close friends and she told me to try a Haakaa. A WHAT? That's what I remember saying to her. I had never heard of that, but I was willing to try anything. Target was three minutes away from me and had some in stock. So, I sent my sons father to grab one. The Haakaa, paired with a hot shower and a breast massage, had the milk flowing in no time. Once again, something the lactation lady failed to mention.

Women have been breastfeeding since the beginning of time. Our bodies just know what to do. For some people, I found that it was hard for them to understand that. People would say "is he getting enough" or "maybe you should supplement." They would think that because I couldn't see how much he was getting that he was somehow lacking. I could literally yell till I was blue in the face that his latching was the demand, and my body would keep up with the supply, but that didn't matter. It was so frustrating. Even at the doctor's appointments they would ask how many ounces he is taking. I wanted to wait until I was at least six weeks postpartum to pump. So, I didn't know the answer. I just knew he was fully satisfied after every feeding.

He was fully satisfied, and I was suffering. I was trying to be comfortable with my new reality and navigate my relationship and all the hormones. But, I was drowning. He was taking everything out of me, and I found myself having to just eat any and everything to just have enough fuel to feed him. I would forget to eat or just didn't feel like making a meal and I was causing myself more harm than good. Whether you exclusively pump or nurse or both, your body needs fuel and hydration, and I was simply not getting what I needed. I started drinking ensure shakes to try and keep myself hydrated. The exhaustion didn't help either. Waiting to pump meant I was the only one who could feed the baby, and I was tired. Our night feeds were the worst, my eyelids would be so heavy, and those fifteen minutes felt like torture. I would let him latch and then hold him and cry.

So many times, I felt like I was failing him. I tried to stay positive and started getting out more with the baby. People would leave the room when the baby started to eat. So, even though I was getting out to help my sanity, I would still end up alone in a room by myself. The first few months were isolating and lonely. I was angry that it was 2022 and breastfeeding was still controversial. People still expected you to go somewhere else as if you were doing something wrong. Like seriously, feeding a baby with a cover over them is like fighting a bull. They want to see. They get hot. You get hot. I was over it. I wasn't trying to please other people. I eventually stopped caring how it made other people feel. I was covered up and what my child was doing was perfectly normal. My mental health was suffering. So, I chose me.

Once I started to pump it was a relief to let someone else feed the baby. But in the end, I ended up choosing to just nurse because I still had to pump. It just felt like double work. Cleaning pump parts was never ending, and it was starting to get on my nerves. It started to weigh on me that I only had a small stash of milk for outings.

Comparison is the thief of joy and I had to limit my social media usage due to constantly seeing posts of women with all this milk in their freezer, or who seemed to be thriving during their postpartum period. Here I was with all these insecurities, especially about not having enough milk. Then, I remember my cousin telling me that if I was pumping the amount of milk my baby typically drinks during a feed, I was doing good. That lifted my spirits a little, but I was ready for a change. I was at my wits end. I didn't want to breastfeed anymore. I was tired of having to wear nurse friendly tops and I wanted to feel cute again. My breasts had changed during my pregnancy, but I started to notice they were getting back to what they looked like pre baby. I still wasn't satisfied with my body and was not allowing myself any grace. After praying about it, I decided to push through and keep breastfeeding. When people would ask me how long I was planning on breastfeeding, my answer was always "I'm taking it a day at a time."

Stress is the number one killer of milk supply. When I was around five months postpartum I noticed a dip in my supply. I tried everything from lactation cookies to body armour drinks as well as different teas. Nothing seemed to work and I had to start supplementing with formula. I felt like such a failure. I was mad that I allowed myself to "feel" because that is what was causing me stress, and now my baby was suffering because of it. My stress was coming from everywhere and I was desperately in need of a good night's rest. I worked from home, so I never really got a break, and I was literally working around the clock. I would get off work and still had to work at being a mom. It was never-ending. My son's father was an hour and a half away due to his job, but I needed a break!

I mustered up the strength to leave my baby and fly across the world to London for a few days, and I remember my friends laughing at me because I was getting my naps in whenever I could. It felt good to not have to be needed for a few days. I was rejuvenated when I came back, and I had a lot of milk for my baby. I was ready to kick the formula. But, unfortunately for me, that never happened. I went back to breast milk for a while, but my stress wasn't gone, and my moment of bliss was just that, a moment! My cycle came back at six months postpartum, and that's when I knew I would not be able to exclusively breastfeed anymore. I had work stress, family stress, friendship stress and postpartum stress.

All of this was killing my supply and building my supply back up was going to take too much work. I didn't have the time or mental capacity to deal with that. The baby was getting bigger and now on solids and purees. He still needed his milk, and I just couldn't satisfy him. I found a formula that worked for my baby. My decision was to nurse at night and the first feed of the day. Then, use the formula during the day. To my surprise I started to feel better with supplementing because I could now let family members or friends keep the baby, a luxury I didn't really have before. I no longer had to limit my time out to run errands, because I was able to make a bottle for him versus pull over in the nearest parking lot and nurse. He was happy and fed. Honestly, that's all that mattered.

It's crazy because I went from being a teenager who barely knew anything about breastfeeding to an adult who felt shamed when having to make a formula bottle in public because I felt judged. I would wonder what was going through other mommy's minds when they saw me making a bottle. Did they think I was lazy? Did they think I didn't try to nurse? So much shame and anxiety for no reason. My son is eleven months now and I still give him my breast from time to time, but I haven't picked up my pump in a month. I'm not sure how much he is getting, but I know it's not much. They don't leak anymore, and he often slaps them when I nurse as if he is trying to get the milk to come out faster. It's actually quite funny. I'm no longer stressed. He loves his plant-based formula, and he doesn't need as much milk anymore anyways because he loves food. This journey is coming to an end and I'm sad that it is over. But, I'm so grateful for the time we had. Our bond is like no other. I feel like I can do anything.

I trusted my body and she did exactly what she needed to do. I was able to nourish my child and nurture him. Having to supplement added to my workload because now I have so many bottles to clean daily. But, I finally found the one thing that I needed in my fourth trimester: grace. I stopped beating myself up. I accepted my body. While I want the loose skin to go away, it's a reminder that I carried a human inside me. That's crazy! So many nights I laid down and watched my baby nurse to sleep, and the way he would hold me or look up at me would calm my anxiety. He needed me and I needed him. For eleven months, we have been helping each other. I might have been sick once and he never caught it. That's amazing. We've had no doctor's visits outside of his routine checkups. Could have just been genetics, or it could have been due to my antibodies helping to protect him. This journey was hard and long, and I probably will never do it again (give me formula and a baby brezza for the next one). But, I learned so much about myself and my body that I wouldn't trade this experience for anything.

I do want more black women to have the opportunity to breastfeed. We need more clinics in our neighborhoods that offer lactation classes. We need systemic racism to stop coming into our hospital rooms. They assume we want formula, and depending on where we deliver, they don't even try to help us get the baby to latch. We need more peer support. If I didn't have my cousin or some of my other friends who had babies before me, breastfeeding may not have been my choice. They showed me it's possible to work and feed my baby. They helped me get comfortable with the idea of it. Now, I make sure I encouraged my friends who have babies after me to at least try. I also make sure they know there is nothing wrong with formula.

The mom shaming must end. Being a parent is hard enough without having all the unnecessary opinions and added stress from other women. I'm not ashamed to say I am relieved that I am at the finish line. I know there are plenty of women who regret weaning and don't look forward to not being able to breastfeed. If you're one of those people, its okay. Go until you're ready. Especially, if your body allows you to. If you're like me and you can taste the relief, then high five sis! Let's have a nursing bra burning party. The version of me that existed before I had the baby is gone and I'm finally excited to really get to know this new version of me. She is powerful and capable. I'm most excited to get rid of my tank tops and camisoles and anything that was made for nursing, so seriously let's burn this stuff. I can't wait to wear a fitted dress that has no access to my breasts or a turtleneck this winter. It's time to activate my sexy. Quad, I love you so much and I just want to say thank you for choosing me to be your mom and being such an awesome teammate on this journey. In a few months to a year you probably won't even remember our nursing sessions but I will never forget. You and your older brother, Que, both came to me when I needed you most. Thank you for giving me a reason to live and a new appreciation of self by helping me realize how capable and strong I really am. Breastfeeding: thank you, NEXT!

Chapter 7

Postpartum Depression

Quantisha Oliver

Hey Mamas!

When you google postpartum depression, we learn that is is depression suffered by a mother following childbirth, typically arising from the combination of hormonal changes, sociological adjustment to motherhood, and fatigue.

Postpartum depression is something that is not talked about enough. There are instances where mothers have taken their own lives, and the tragedy is not only the life lost, but the fact that their children are growing up without a mom. For so many years women have suffered in silence. Mothers have taken their lives prematurely, children have been abused, children have been abandoned, in so many other awful things because the mothers did not know how to ask for help, and I am no different.

My story starts with me being diagnosed with polycystic ovary syndrome when I was sixteen years old. Polycystic ovary syndrome (PCOS) is a condition in which the ovaries produce an abnormal amount of androgens (male sex hormones) that are usually present in women in small amounts. The name polycystic ovary syndrome describes the numerous small cysts that form in the ovaries.

Polycystic ovary syndrome is a hormonal imbalance that causes so many changes to go on in the female body. Despite the many challenges I had as a child with abnormal bleeding, mood swings, constant weight changes, skin issues and so much more, I made the best out of life. I was outgoing, never afraid to take risk, and a lot of fun to be around.

I was told at a young age that I would never have children "naturally", and I should probably think about fertility treatments if I ever desired to be a mother. So, you can imagine what it felt like as a sixteen year old getting this type of news.

At sixteen years old, motherhood was the furthest thing from my mind. But, sometimes when I laid in bed at night, I would have thoughts about what my life would be like with or without children.

Fast forward to my adult life...

My husband and I tried for a few years to conceive. I was holding on to this "secret" that I wasn't ready to share, which left my husband wondering if something was wrong with him. We were tracking my periods and trying to track ovulation. But, there was still something very important I had not shared with him. I eventually got the courage to sit down and share with him my diagnosis of PCOS at the age of sixteen. I then went on to share with him that it would be extremely hard for me to conceive a child without taking fertility medications. We are people of faith. So, when I shared this news with my husband, he immediately began to pray for me. I realized I had to come to terms and face the reality that my husband really wanted a child with me, and I may never be able to give him that.

Little did we know, I was already two months pregnant. I went into my doctor to talk about my options with fertility medication and the nurse came into the room with tears in her eyes. I thought that maybe something was wrong. So, I instantly became worried. The nurse stood in front of me and said, "I have an amazing surprise for you!" I looked at her and I said," Okay, what's the surprise?" She replied," You're pregnant!" I thought that maybe she was playing a joke on me. So, I sat there in disbelief while holding the pregnancy test in my hand.

The test was positive. But, because I never thought this would be my reality, it was hard for me to accept. My nurse looked at me and asked "Are you excited?" I replied "I don't know how I feel right now. This doesn't feel real." She went on to say "Okay, I certainly understand. I'll go get the doctor to do an ultrasound to find out how far along you are."

I called my husband and I told him," Baby, we're pregnant!" He thought I was playing a sick prank on him due to our conversation only one week ago. So, he asked for proof. I was a little offended at first. But, I had to remember the news I shared with him about my diagnosis.

Finally, the doctor came into the room. She turned off the lights and did the vaginal ultrasound. There it was, the heartbeat of my little peanut. I began to cry tears of joy! My doctor grabbed my hands and said "You did it! Wooo Hooo!" I replied," Yes, we did it!"

I couldn't hold the news any longer, I began calling everyone while she was still doing the ultrasound. I got my husband back on the phone to show him that we finally did it. He asked how far along we were, and the doctor replied," She's eleven weeks pregnant, and her chances of a miscarriage are very low. Your little peanut has a strong heartbeat!"

I couldn't believe it! I'm finally going to be a mom! When I hung up with my husband I called my mom to share the news with her. She was so excited she couldn't even speak. Before I could call anyone else, a mass text went out, and my whole family knew! The power of technology is something else. LOL!

I had a pretty good pregnancy up until week twenty. That's when we found out that I had an anterior placenta. This occurs when the placenta grows in the front of the uterine wall, which makes it hard to feel your baby's kicks and find the baby's heartbeat.

It was hard for me to feel peanut kicking or moving. So, I was on edge from week twenty up until it was time to push him out. By week twenty-seven, we found out that my cervix was open. At the time, I was working a lot to prepare my finances to bring a new life into the world. Immediately after the ultrasound, my doctor put me on mandatory bed rest for the remainder of my pregnancy. This news was very worrisome. But, I had an amazing doctor and I trusted her opinion. So, I knew that she wouldn't steer me wrong.

My husband told me not to worry and that he would take good care of us. The main focus was bringing peanut into this world strong and healthy. So, bed rest was my reality and I had to be okay with that. Instead of enjoying sunlight and taking cute little maternity pictures, I was in the house resting on my back, reading books and studying on how to be a good mother. Each time I went into my doctor's office, she would reassure me that everything was fine. At the visits, I would be able to see him moving (and he was super-busy).

His heartbeat remained strong the entire pregnancy. Due to my cervix being open I had to be induced at 37 weeks. It wasn't ideal, but it was a precaution. I tried my best to be strong without an epidural. But, as soon as the first contraction came I screamed for the doctor to give me an epidural. I'll never forget that feeling, and I applaud all mothers that have natural births. That takes a different type of strength!

I pushed a total of ten times and we finally welcomed peanut into the world. He's no longer peanut; his new identity is King. We chose to name him King to remind him of his inner strength. Even though I put having children in the back of my mind, I always said that if I'm ever blessed to have children, I want them to have names of strength, courage and wisdom.

King is finally here and reality hits! As soon as I got in the car and looked at our son my first feelings were feelings of fear! I didn't do well with breastfeeding in the hospital. So, I feared I wouldn't be able to feed my child.

I had to look into my options of formula feeding our baby and that made me feel horrible. I couldn't shake the feeling that although our child is being fed he wasn't being fed the way that I wanted to feed him. So, I instantly began my new experience as a new mom seeing myself as less than, because my body wasn't producing the way I thought that it should. Little did I know, this was the start of postpartum depression for me.

Having a baby is a joyous time and it's also celebrated in so many ways. But, one thing no one really talks about is what happens after the baby arrives: the body changes that we go through and the mental toll it takes on us. Some moms even experience very dark phases where they feel like they're sinking into a dark hole. This phase after birth it's called postpartum depression. I can remember a time after I had my son that everyone around me was rejoicing except for me. The only thing I could think about were things that could go wrong. Like, what if I'm not a good mom? What if I leave my baby with him or her and they hurt my child? What if my husband leaves me? What if I wake up one day and my baby's not breathing? I can remember going into the bathroom and crying my heart out because I was afraid of being a mom. But, as time went on I realized that I wasn't afraid of being a mom, I was afraid of failing as a mom.

After having my son, I heard so many voices in my head telling me that I'm not going to be a good mom, and that I should give my son up for adoption. My husband and I were on the verge of divorce. So, dealing with all of that pressure on top of being a new mom, balancing a business, being a youth mentor and a youth minister, can you imagine the weight that was on my shoulders? There were days where I would just lay in bed and my son would be screaming to the top of his lungs. I would tell myself "you're going to be okay" and "you've got this". But, the truth was I was not okay and I didn't have it all together.

I thought about so many ways to end my life, and I thought about so many different ways I could run away. My son has the best godparents a kid could ever have. So, in my mind, if I took my own life King would be raised and brought up with love, a strong village, and stability. I can remember waking up one morning and telling myself that I had to shake this feeling that I was feeling. There is no way that God would bless me with such an amazing and precious gift for me not to love, cherish, and nurture him. I had to muster up all the strength that I had to fight this depression. I would be lying if I said it was easy. But, with each passing day things got better and I got stronger. I was determined to change my mindset, and to fight back against these thoughts and feelings that I was having. I was determined to be the best mother I could be.

We prepare ourselves for so many things: leadership, college, relationships and more. But, we can never truly prepare ourselves for parenthood. We can take parenting classes, read books and listen to our elders. But, when our precious gifts arrive, and we look them in the eyes, everything we've read, studied, and all the stories we've heard go out the window. What we realize is that our children are unique and need a tailor made care plan with the most important ingredient: unconditional love.

I had everyone's opinion, thoughts, and concerns imprinted in my heart and mind. At that stage in my life, I was an over thinker. So, everything someone told me was overanalyzed, and my brain was going haywire. It is very important for new moms to find their voice and find their identity. Every morning that you wake up encourage yourself, affirm yourself, and most of all believe in yourself. There is absolutely nothing wrong with getting advice from other moms. Just remember that when your precious jewel is here with you that he or she will need a special care plan that comes straight from your heart to theirs.

During my battle with postpartum depression I had to dig deep to find my strength again. I have an amazing husband that helped me through this journey, and my mother was always just a phone call away, willing to listen as I talked to her about things I was worried about. I also had a mentor I called who prayed me through many nights when I wanted to give up because things had gotten so hard for me. I was in such a dark place. I thought that I would never come out of this. But, I'm still here! I fought my way out of that depression. I learned to affirm my day, affirm myself, and always think positive. I looked in the mirror everyday and I told myself "you're beautiful, you're smart, you're a great mother, you're strong, you're bold, you're courageous, you're a life changer, and your life matters!"

Anything negative was completely erased out of my life. Allowing negative things to stay connected to you will weigh you down in ways that you can't even imagine. You have the power to control your atmosphere. So, don't be afraid to choose your sanity over what you're familiar with! It's important during this phase of your life to choose you and your mental health over anything else.

You're going to have to develop a plan of escape out of this darkness and back into the light.

Overcoming postpartum depression takes a lot of strength, courage and wisdom. Your strength comes from knowing and understanding what you're going through doesn't define you. Muster up the strength to keep pressing, to keep fighting, and to keep going. The courage comes from within during your weakest moments to fight back against all of these mental struggles and setbacks. Lastly, the wisdom comes from putting all of this together in developing a plan to conquer this season of your life. Where you are and who you are now is not where you will be or who you will be in the near future!

In this new journey you're going to face challenging things. So, it's very important that you learn to adjust and listen to your body when you feel exhausted. It's okay to take a moment to breathe. Eating well also goes hand in hand with listening to your body. The things you eat plays a big part in the way you feel. If you're feeling sad and depressed, don't turn to emotional eating. Figure out alternative snacks that help with keeping the body healthy.

During your recovery, you may feel tired, overwhelmed, stressed, and may even experience loss of identity. In these intense moments of pressure, rest as much as you possibly can. Don't put pressure on yourself. Talk with family and friends about how you're feeling. It's very important that you don't bottle up your feelings. Feel what you feel and continue to press on.

When you change the way that you look at things, the things around you will change. But don't beat yourself up during your season of transformation. You won't have victory overnight. But, as long as you continue to show up for yourself, you prove to yourself everyday that you are stronger than you were yesterday. As you grow stronger, you will start to see that you have the power and the authority to fight a bigger obstacle than you think you were able to fight before.

After every storm a rainbow appears. I know it may seem like this storm will never end for you. But, I promise you, as long as you stay faithful to yourself, remain true to who you are, and fight like you've never fought before, you will get through this. I stand as a testimony to this fact!

If you're a mommy that doesn't know where to go for help, please know that there is help out there for you! Start with your doctor, and make sure your immediate family knows how you're feeling.

I share my postpartum story with no shame and no regret, because I believe that sharing my story will help others who are going through. Don't be afraid to seek help. Your little miracle deserves that and you owe it to yourself to come out of this!

Chapter 8

Guilty As Charged

Amber D. Brown-Jones

The burden of not feeling secure about pouring my heart and soul into someone has always been a burden on my shoulders. When I was younger, I thought having a baby was about finally having someone I could love, and who would be able to love me unconditionally. However, I was wrong. It was so much more. Forget about having to buy clothes, shoes, and food for a second. Nobody told me beforehand how much I would have to sacrifice for us to survive anyway. We need to talk about how no one spoke about the mental stressors or trauma a mother must bear before and after giving birth. As with my life path, I had to learn it the hard way.

Now, when it comes to what others say, my nature is not the type to necessarily value opinions to a certain extent. It is especially true if they have never gone through what I have. So, trust me when I say I know what I am talking about.

I was unsure what to do or think when I found out I was pregnant with my oldest child. I sat on the edge of the bed and stared at myself in the mirror for about thirty minutes or so. I guess reality started to sink in gradually because questions began to form in my head. Was I really pregnant? How did it happen? I thought I couldn't get pregnant, and I worried about what everyone would think about me once they found out the news. I worried about what the family of my past relationships would think. I wondered if they would feel like I betrayed or stepped out on their son/brother. What about my family, especially my dad? How would he feel once he found out I was pregnant? I compared my situation to my sister's, knowing the disappointment my dad felt for her not only having children, but the type of guy she got pregnant by. There was very little difference between her kid's father and the type of guy I chose. Depending on how you looked at it, some might consider those types as street-wise men or drug dealers. But I just saw a challenge, happiness, and excitement. I also thought about what my child's father would think. Was he going to be happy when I told him? Would he want me to get an abortion? Was he going to deny that the baby was his? We broke up a month or so before I found out I was pregnant. I was happy and definitely planning on telling him, because I missed him and was too prideful to tell him. Secretly, it was a blended feeling of I'm scared, but I got him, or he's mine now, or the known saying of I'm not going anywhere. At that time, I was young and ignorant, so please try not to judge me. There's probably still grown woman who still hold that belief. I'm merely saying! Anyway, after reaching out to his sister through social media and sending her my number for him to call me, I was finally able to speak with him to tell him the news. My heart was beating out of my chest, and because I'm a chronic over thinker, I automatically assumed he would feel like the baby did not belong to him. I mean, logically, a person would have thought that, no? As I mentioned, a full month had passed since the breakup, and because I'm such an over-thinker I already assumed he would feel like the baby did not belong to him. You know the famous questions men ask, "Who have you been having sex with?" or "Am I the only one you were with?". I think I just wanted to prepare myself for the worse before he asked so I wouldn't get offended.

During the conversation, I mentioned to him that I was willing to get an abortion if he wanted me to or if he wanted a DNA test before signing the birth certificate. At that moment, it was all about whatever I needed to say so he could feel that level of security in knowing the child was his growing inside me. Truthfully, in my heart, I wanted to keep my baby, but I still wanted to be fair in the situation.

When I was young, I remember a female tried to convince my cousin that her children were his. My aunt (his mother) was not going for it. She made him pressure her for a DNA test, and it turned out that the babies were not his. That situation sticks with me even to this day. I imagined how embarrassed she must've been and thought that I would never put myself in that type of predicament. Not only her, but my cousin's feelings were hurt. The look on his face said it all, but he never mentioned it again.

Now fast forward because this is not even the best part of what I want to tell you. On July 5, 2012, I gave birth to a beautiful seven pound, four ounce baby boy. I guess the father of my son was confident that was his child, because he did not hesitate to sign his name on the birth certificate paperwork. You probably think how great it was that things turned out well for me, and maybe that made things better for us. I wish I could say I was happy, but I was not. As I held my son for the first time in my arms, embracing his pureness and affectionately crying over the joyous love I developed immediately for him, guilt consumed me for the first time. My mind began to fill with negative thoughts. I felt so guilty for ever feeling or thinking of getting an abortion, and for caring about other people's opinions. All I could do was hug my son, rub my nose across his face, cry, and apologize to him even though I knew he didn't understand.

As I was going through all this, I failed to recognize it was something I needed to bring to someone's attention. I typically expressed my emotions when no one was around. It was just me and my baby alone together. He was the only one I would talk to. As a result, I found it possible to be in my most authentic, vulnerable, wholehearted self with my son. Instead of speaking about how I felt to an adult, I just held it in the whole time, and that did so much damage to me mentally. For a long time, I would beat myself up about my past thoughts. Eventually, I began thinking I was a bad mom because of it. This guilt was more powerful that the guilt I felt about my thoughts of getting rid of my son. I also got to a point where I had to pick and choose who and what was more important: work, school, or my son. I understand now why it is so important to have children when your life is more stable because having a child at a young age, and still trying to experience life and establish yourself is not for the weak. Hear me out, please. You will get to a point where you will have to pick and choose who or what is more important. Now or later. I consider the term "now" as physically being there to raise your child and make those memories, and the term "later" as sacrificing those memories to be financially stable to take care of your child eventually. My choice was to focus on going to school, so I can get a degree while working a nine to five. Maybe for you, it would be working to save up enough money to put a down payment on your own home, or just working to afford diapers. Deliberately, I chose the "later" financial route. Logically, it was the best decision at that time. I thought that if I became financially stable, by default, my son would have been as well. The sacrifices I made then, he would have understood later when he got older. My point is not to say I was right or wrong in my decision. I'm just saying it contributed to the guilt I was nurturing. I felt like I wasn't a good mother because I wasn't always present in my son's life. I felt guilty about all the times my son was looking for me to be there, and I couldn't because I had to work. I remember one day, after stopping by my cousin's house on my way home, she was on the phone with her mom. Me being polite, I spoke to her, and in return, she asked me, "What are you doing over there? You ought to have been home with your child"! Now when I tell you, that made me feel so low. My cousin saw the emotions all over my face. She was even offended by what her mom said to me. Granted, she never apologized for it. But, I figured it was a heavy topic and awkward to discuss, which is why I eventually let it go. Another guilt moment for me was when my son accidentally hurt himself. Of course, in the walking stage, children sometimes fall and hurt themselves, but the fact that my son got up crying and ran to my mom for comfort triggered a hurtful feeling inside of me. At that moment, I realized that he looked at her more as a mother figure than he did me, and the only one to blame was me for my sacrificial absence. For years, it was a fight in transitioning him to seeing me as his go-to or primary protector. He is eleven now, and he knows I will protect him. Yet, I will never be able to break the bond he formed with my mother in my absence. Not to say I would want him to do that anyway. My mom is the absolute best grandmother a kid could ask for. I truly love and appreciate everything she has done for my son and myself. She was always the backbone I didn't realize I always had and still have.

On September 8, 2022, eight pounds and twelve ounces later, we had another son. I reached a turning point in my life by the time he was born. Can you guess what I tried to do? If you were to assume that I was trying to correct all the poor decisions I made with my first son, then you would be correct. I figured after making poor decisions in the past, I should try to do things differently. But, guess how that also caused me to feel? Guilty. Let me start by saying that my second son was also an unplanned child. In my mind, I kept my son as a means of retaliation against my first child's father. We called it quits, and when he realized I was serious, he started impregnating different women. Our relationship has always had this unspoken understanding. Something that did not require an explanation. Because there was no turning back, we just knew which boundaries were never to be crossed, and we crossed them to hurt one another. I would assume that the possibility of turning back was there because we were still hurting each other by stepping across those unforgivable boundaries and rubbing it in each other's faces. Either way, I can only assume, but I will never know officially, being that I'm married now, and my son's father was shot and killed in 2021.

Another reason why I kept my baby was because I had gone through two abortions, and I was not trying to put my body through that trauma again. I secretly called my second son my revenge baby. I told you before don't judge me as I speak my truth. They say you are your worse enemy and your worse critic. So, there is nothing I haven't said to myself that you may be thinking right about now.

There was no memorable moment for me, no happy feeling when I found out I was pregnant with my second son. I felt guilty about my secrets throughout my pregnancy, not just for the baby but for my husband. He didn't deserve that. He did not ask for that. I guess that's what baggage means because I had more than the carousels at the airports. As a result of my deep-seated guilt, I became the worst version of myself. I chose to keep it all in and fight through it, but it destroyed me gradually. I cried often and felt like I took my frustration out on others. For example, my first son. Now being the oldest sibling of my two younger sisters, you would think I would know better. Being the trial-and-error child, why would I put my son in that same position? In those circumstances, I felt likeI was out of control. I remember how emotionally stressed out my oldest son was after witnessing my postpartum depression stage after I had my second son.

When COVID was in full swing, I worked remotely from home. I dealt with the drama of my customer service job. Especially, customers being rude because my baby would be crying in the background. On one of the calls, the customer repeatedly said, "Ma'am, I cannot hear you." My reaction was to take my baby to his room, close the door, and then return to the phone. To this, he responded "Wow". Even though we could communicate better, he could still hear my baby crying and banging on the door in the background. Toward the end of our conversation, I apologized on behalf of my baby. He replied, "Ma'am, you are a mother, and I respect you for doing what you are doing, trying to work and provide for your child. If you need to take a moment for your baby, this job should not matter because it can wait. It is ok. We are all in a pandemic, and if people do not understand, that's their problem". I felt that was God's way of speaking to me through my customer. I cried because what I did was wrong, and it was a message he knew I needed at the time. How could I allow myself to leave my baby in his room and let him figure it out for himself? Although he was safe on the floor, in a clean room with toys to keep him company, I failed to understand he was alone and scared in that moment. I was too overwhelmed to think correctly. I didn't think about it. I just did it. Despite his best efforts, my eight-year-old had trouble focusing on his virtual learning classes. He had an excuse for not being able to concentrate most of the time, so using the term best is a stretch. I also found moving into my first house and settling in was quite stressful. Due to my lack of knowledge about dogs and animals, I had to put my husband's dog outside, and I did not have time to pay her any attention. As a result, she barked every time I left her in the backyard, and eventually, the neighbors called the cops or animal control on me because of the noise. My husband had was deployed and she had become accustomed to him being around, playing with her, and loving her. Being a single parent then, I had no choice but to leave her alone. I didn't have the time for the dog. My responsibilities included handling the kids, finances, and accounts, which included paying bills on time. Not to mention cooking, housekeeping, and laundry. You understand what I am trying to say. Things were overwhelming.

I felt guilty for treating my first son like an emotional punching bag. As much as he loved me, I abused his emotions, making him fear me instead. I remember moments when he cried because he was so confused about not knowing what he was supposed to do to help me or what I wanted from him. At one point, I noticed stress bags under his eyes while looking at him. My triggers often felt like another side of me was taking over, and I had no control over them. But that is no excuse. He was only eight. What did he need to do? Everything was my fault: I found myself guilty, knowing I could never erase those moments from his memories, I felt remorseful about hurting my first love and putting things on his plate that were never his responsibility, I felt guilty for yelling at both of my boys ad the times I stormed out of the house because my baby would not stop crying. While they were alone inside the house, I would sit in my car screaming and kicking, telling myself that I would never have another child. Essentially, I forced my first son to deal with his brother alone. When I eventually came back into the house, my first son would look at me briefly, hoping to see that he made me proud after settling his brother down, and I would ignore him. I would walk past them as if they each did not exist and go to my room. As a mother, I was guilty of putting my work ahead of both of my children and not taking the mental break I needed. It made me feel guilty for not being able to balance my life and ensure my first son got the guidance he needed in his education, even with me knowing I didn't want him to be another static. I was sure the school was thinking that maybe his parents were not involved or did not care about his education. In those moments, I did not know who I was. I definitely knew I wasn't myself, and I was so afraid to open up and tell anyone because I did not want anyone to think I was a neglectful mom, or I did not care about my kids. I also did not desire Child Protective Services to feel they may have needed to intervene when I knew I would give my life for my children.

I hated what I had become, and I still fight being that person. It has been a long journey, and I still have a long way to go. However, I decided to share my experience with you so you know it is not just you. You are not alone, Mama. Sometimes I just wanted to bawl in someone's arms to feel comfort and be able to express myself. It did not matter whether it was a person or God. Yes, I have had those thoughts of ending it all. We do not always receive what we believe we need as mothers, so we must continue to fight. As such, this does not mean it is acceptable, but I am not saying it is incorrect either. If only I knew how to believe in myself and to have faith that everything would work out. I wish I knew it was safe to let my guard down. I wish I knew that I could walk by faith. I wish I knew I had someone to talk to the whole time, as I looked back and reflected on who I am today. I am glad that I was able to go through my trials and tribulations so that I would be able to help another mom. We are the pioneers, and if we learn to support one another, Mama, I know we will be blessed to bask in the fruits of our labor. You got this! Never let anyone tell you otherwise. Mama, I am guilty as charged, but I will always continue persevering and moving forward for my children. In my experience, there is no such thing as a perfect mom. Ultimately, if your situation is like mine, you will have to accept what you cannot control and embrace what you can control, so you can be at peace with how things are. It will not be easy, but each day will bring strength, and you will find yourself again, Mama. There is no harm in shuffling around priorities when it is appropriate and needed. You will be a better version of yourself. The most rewarding part is that you will feel happy again. As someone who has always sacrificed for the greater good, I have developed a bit of tough skin. I would love to be vulnerable (I just got that while sharing with you). I have been able to let my guard down and lift the burden off my shoulders so I can now experience all of what life has to offer me as a mother. We can thrive together, Mama!

Chapter 9

Partner Relationship
Mary K. Purnell

Can you imagine standing in the mirror and not recognizing who you are anymore? Well, there I was, standing in the mirror after two months of becoming a mother, and I had no idea who I was. I was 45 pounds heavier than I was prior to giving birth to my son, and trying to adjust to my new found body while still trying to feel sexy. Sometimes you get lost in the shuffle: hair isn't done, throw up on your shirt, leaky breast and you're too tired to get yourself together.

I had lost myself and didn't even realize it. I had gotten into a routine of caring for this little human being that I just gave birth to that I had not only neglected myself but my partner as well. Trying to remain sexy when you don't feel sexy can become a challenge. Getting back to me was tough and in the midst of that, I lost sight of my relationship.

I remember when our son was five or six months old. My son's father said to me "you just forgot all about me. It's like we had the baby and I do not exist anymore". To hear the man I love and share this life with felt like this, felt like a ton of bricks crushing my heart. This is not something you want to hear from your partner. As his woman, I had to really take a step back and ask myself, had I really become so lost in becoming a mom that I completely forgot about him. The sobering answer was 'yes'. I had to apologize because I had become Mary, the mom. I had lost Mary, the woman. I had his support in the caring for our child. So, what was it? It was great that we were able to talk about it. That conversation put so much into perspective for me, and I knew I had to make some changes. It is hard not to lose yourself after becoming a mother. Recognizing it and making sure you stop at nothing to find her is key.

Protecting and maintaining a healthy relationship with your partner is crucial. After having a baby, the partner relationship sometimes ends because both parties find it hard to adjust to the new individuals you have become. Our relationships suffer as a result of the focus on this new addition to the family. Strengthening your partnership after becoming parents is key to nurturing the relationship with each other. Some ways to do this would be to make sure to date each other. Incorporate a date night at least two to three times a month. Little gestures also go a long way. Plan a picnic with just the two of you, or sending the baby to grandma's house just to sit home, order in, and watch Netflix together. Those alone times allow you two to rebuild and reconnect.

Balancing the roles of partner, mother, sister, daughter, friend, etc. is something people don't discuss very much. But, it's something every woman deals with. Let's face it, all types of relationships suffer tremendously after a baby comes if we don't pay attention and make adjustments.

It's overwhelming being a mom and there are times you will long for the days of feeling like your old self. An open line of communication is key in a relationship after having a baby in order to work together and overcome obstacles. Your partner should know when you're overwhelmed. Don't make him guess how you're feeling. Communicate if you need of a break, and let your partner know how they can support you. What they assume is support may not be what you desire or what you need.

Partner relationships can become trying when the mom feels like they are doing the bulk of caring for the child, and a sense of resentment may form. This can cause a wedge to form between you and your partner. There were times where I wanted to just scream or even hit my child's father, because I felt like I was doing everything. But once I communicated how I felt and allowed him to step in, there was a shift in my mood. I had to also realize that just because he wasn't doing it the way I would do it did not make it wrong.

Being a mom can become inundating to the point where you don't feel like yourself or want to get dressed to go out with your partner. I remember my partner wanting to go out when we were baby free for the weekend. I just did not feel beautiful or want to even attempt to try and pull myself together. Instead of me communicating that, I just simply said 'no'. To him, that came off as me rejecting him and started and unnecessary disagreement. You get in mom mode and do not know how to turn it off. The moment your sweet little baby goes to sleep, all you want to do is shower and curl up in the bed to get some rest. We are not focusing on being sexy for our man. They get what is left of us, which is not a lot after dealing with a crying, fussy infant.

As mothers we focus on protecting and pouring into this little human we created and taking care of ourselves is not our first priority. I can remember days where I did not feel desirable and sexy. Research shows that a fifth of couples break up during the first twelve months after welcoming their babies. People do not like to discuss this, because it can be a touchy topic or you may feel that you are the only one that may be experiencing this. You are not alone. Your relationship will be tested. You may feel like you aren't sexy, and he may feel like you are not focused on him anymore. It comes down to balancing the fact that you now have to incorporate this new little human being into your world. Remembering that you are a team will allow you to become closer and lean on one another as you are embarking on this new journey together.

I started to make sure I took care of myself more to the point where I made myself feel sexy and more desirable. We started to plan more dates, sending the baby to grandma's house and we would spend time in the house together ordering take out and watching our favorite shows. This allowed us to get back to us and decompress from the parental roles. The alone time helped us tremendously. I appreciated the small things that we were able to rekindle when we would spend weekends without our son. It allowed me to rekindle my relationship with Mary.

During this time it was refreshing for not only me but for us as a whole. In these small moments I found myself being more appreciative of our relationship. Having the support system outside of you and your partner is imperative. You will need your village when you need your alone time to unwind, while having the piece of mind that your baby is safe. Our village was extremely crucial for us as we got back to the two individuals that fell in love to create this beautiful little boy.

Understanding that you are a woman as well as a mother and knowing how to separate the two is a key element to staying grounded and not losing yourself in becoming a new mom. It is most certainly easier said than done, ensuring that you find the balance can be hard. Trust me I know. I wish I had a group of women that would have told me how easy it is lose yourself when becoming a mom. I believe knowing that you are not the same woman that you were before you had the baby will allow you to embrace the new woman you have become.

Many times we don't want to accept that we are not a size six or eight anymore. And we often begin to compare ourselves to how our "snapback" should be that we do not feel sexy about our new mom bodies. As a woman when you don't feel sexy you don't want to be bothered or feel like going the extra mile to be sexy. Not feeling desirable as a woman is something that everyone nine times out of ten will feel after becoming a mom. This has nothing to do with your partner, for me it was coming to terms that I was no longer the Mary I was.

Partner Relationships are tested the most when the baby comes. However, it does not mean that they will fail, or that you can't overcome and become a stronger couple. Communication is imperative to overcoming the trials and obstacles that you and your partner may face. However, it is important to remember that there is no manual or formula. If you communicate and work as a team it will allow not only a healthy parenting relationship, but it will also strengthen your relationship that you had prior to the baby.

As a mother, knowing you have the support of your partner is refreshing. Knowing that when your he comes home from work, although he may be tired, is going to get the baby for a little while because he understands and knows you need a break. It's not only calming for me, but also a turn on. Women are naturally nurturing, and it is our natural instinct to nurture and assume all the responsibilities of the baby. We don't understand until we're exhausted, how draining it is to do everything ourselves. Having a supportive partner is crucial to having a healthy relationship after the baby comes.

Whether we prepare for it or not, a shift in the relationship is going to happen. The type of shift is up to you and your partner. So, before the baby comes, express your concerns. Becoming a parent is a beautiful thing that many people do not get the honor to experience, whether it is by choice or not. So don't allow something that is so beautiful turn you and your partner's relationship into something that is not so beautiful.

For me, the transitional aspect of me being Mary, the mom and Mary, the woman was something that I had an extremely hard time balancing. For a long time, I thought that there was something wrong with me. It's hard not to see these women on social media and not compare yourself to how fast they "snapped" back. I had to ask myself, who's taking care of their kids, and is this "snap back" natural? The answer: there's probably a nanny and nine times out of ten probably not. Comparison is probably the worst thing you can do after becoming a mom. Your journey is completely different than everyone else's.

The sooner you're able to embrace your new body the sooner you will be able to begin to love the new you. While it is crucial to have the support of your spouse, they can't make you love your new body. That has to come from within. Often times we look for reassurance from our spouse that even when they give it to us it is not enough because we have not embrace our new body.

Before having our son, I thought I had the perfect body. I ate what I wanted and didn't gain a pound. I was 140-145 pounds and gained 60 plus pounds with my son. Lord!!! And after I gave birth I looked in the mirror and said "why do I still look pregnant?" I remember my mom looking at me and laughing. She said, "It will go down, Mary. You just had a baby". All I was thinking to myself is "when?" Without me even knowing it, I was rejecting the new me. As time went on, I lost maybe 10-15 pounds from nursing, and I thank God everyday for that.

Even with the reassurance it wasn't enough for me because I wasn't ready to accept that I wasn't that 25-year-old with the flat stomach. I had a little bit more now. So that's when the insecurities creep in, because you're not feeling sexy anymore. I got so comfortable with just being mom because it was easier than being both. Often we get caught up in what is easier for us and shy away from what will be a challenge. Mommies, I am here to tell you that embracing your new self and finding the balance of being a woman and mom is a challenge. But guess the fuck what????? You got this. YOU WERE BUILT FOR THIS!!! Some days you will feel like the sexiest woman on earth and some days you feel like crap. But both days should be embraced.

I learned that once my partner let me know that he felt pushed to the side, it wasn't because I didn't want him it was because I still was trying to find me. Finding yourself again is not easy, takes courage, and is scary as shit. But, it is worth it. Get dressed and go out, and not just with your partner. Go out with your girlfriends, too. Pouring into you is needed to get your "mojo" back. Talk to your partner about how you're feeling on the days you're just overwhelmed and don't want to see another bottle, diaper or wipe. Often times, we want to be super woman because we feel like we can. Then, we are mad at our partner when we feel like we're not getting as much help as we want.

The times when I was able to sleep in more and something as simple as take a shower, I was grateful. To know that my son was okay while I took care of myself, because he was with his dad, made me happy. Guess what else it did? It made me want my partner that much more. I'm not sure about y'all, but a man being a father is a huge turn on. Anytime I was able to get thirty more minutes of sleep, I'd look at him and say, "I got something special for you tonight". It truly is the little things that matter so much when we are new moms. So, when you get that extra thirty minutes of sleep or able to take that long bath, appreciate it.

The testing of a lot of relationships is we forget to appreciate each other. Both can sometimes get in the head space of "that is what you're supposed to do". While having a child responsibilities attached, you're still suppose to appreciate one another and what you do to make life easier for the family as a whole. When this sense of appreciation isn't there, resentment takes it places. When resentment comes in, it will fester when there is no communication.

You all worked together to create this beautiful life and should work together to nurture this little human being. There is no such thing as this is what mom is supposed to or this is what dad is supposed to do. You are a team. When someone isn't pulling their weight communicate that. The relationship you have with your partner is important, and just because you are parents it should not suffer. Nobody's role is more or less important than the other one.

One conversation with my partner changed my complete outlook on everything. The scariest thing is that I had got so caught up in being a mom that I had not even noticed that I no longer was Mary, the woman. It is so easy to fall into this trap. No one prepared me for what I was feeling, and no one could. Although, I do wish I had known that after a baby your relationship is tested. No one told me "Mary some days you won't feel sexy, and it can affect how you interact with your partner". I was going through it and didn't even realize it. One conversation shifted everything for me which cause me to reflect and ask myself questions. I asked myself some hard questions, and it all went back to me simply not embracing this new woman I was. Once I realized "You're not 25-year old Mary with the flat stomach anymore. You're 26-year old Mary with a lil bit more but guess what YOU'RE STILL THE SHIT". Baby!! It was a game changer!

Getting the relationship back with the new you will give power and confidence to know that you are sexy, and desirable.

102

Some days you may not feel as fine as the day before and that is okay. Establishing this relationship will help strengthen the one with your partner, as well as having that open line of communication.

Relationships are hard and take work when it's just the two of you. But, keeping in mind that you are a team and should tackle parenthood as a team will help you both. Not expecting one parent to do more is important. One parent is not more responsible than the other. The well-being of the baby is both parents job.

Mommies, fall back in love with yourself after your baby, establish that relationship again. Tell yourselves "I'm fine", "I'm sexy" and believe it. So when you hear it from your partner it's like "oh you've noticed it to, huh"!! It is a challenge but you can do it. You are beautiful even with extra weight, the leaky breasts, and the vomit on you shirt. You are still SEXY!!! You're just a SEXY MOM!!! You are not the same woman you were before you had the baby. Now you are even more resilient and wonderful! Your partnership will be tested, but you got this!! You just brought a beautiful life into this world nothing can stop you from accomplishing anything!!!

Chapter 10

Returning to Work

Whitney Moody

A djusting to life with a newborn is an exhilarating and challenging experience. After spending a week or two at home, and getting into a rhythm with your little one, it's time to navigate the next big step: returning to work. Suddenly, your schedule must accommodate not just your own needs, but also those of your baby. The complexity intensifies as you delve into the world of childcare arrangements. Who will be entrusted with the care of your precious child while you're at work? Will it be a family member, a trusted friend, or a daycare facility? As you consider these options, the financial aspect also comes into play, as childcare expenses become a new consideration.

Preparing for your return to work involves more than just finding the right caregiver. You'll need to gather a host of essentials for your baby, whether it's for the day or the entire week. Are you opting for formula feeding or planning to pump breast milk while at work? Determining the amount of formula to send with your baby each day adds another layer of planning. These are just a few of the many questions that arise when contemplating a return to the workforce. And that's not all.

The intricacies continue as you factor in your work schedule, coordinating drop-offs and pickups, and assessing whether your workplace provides a suitable space for pumping and storing breast milk. Amidst all these considerations, time feels limited, and the pressure to adequately plan looms large. The journey back to work is multifaceted, demanding careful thought and organization.

The moment I laid eyes on my baby, a mix of emotions swept over me—joy and happiness intertwined with fear and confusion. Seeing the face of the little one I had nurtured within me for nine months was a profoundly moving experience. However, the reality of being solely responsible for this tiny life, entrusted to me by the doctors, shattered the plans and expectations I had meticulously crafted. Suddenly, my well-thought-out strategies seemed obsolete, and I found myself navigating parenthood on an hour-by-hour, day-by-day basis.

All the preparation, the countless hours of reading, researching, and watching YouTube videos on infant care seemed to pale in comparison to the actual task at hand. It was as if I had walked into the hospital on the day of my baby's birth with a blank slate, realizing that my knowledge was merely theoretical and that real-life situations demanded an entirely new level of understanding.

The truth was that no amount of research or external advice could have fully prepared me for the intricacies of caring for my son. The transition from envisioning a well-structured plan to the unpredictable reality of caring for a newborn was a jarring awakening. I found myself grappling with a multitude of questions and uncertainties, questioning my own readiness, and feeling somewhat overwhelmed.

It was a humbling realization that parenthood is a continuous learning process—one that cannot be entirely mastered through books or online resources. The sheer magnitude of responsibility and the depth of love and care required for this small, vulnerable human being were far more profound than I had anticipated. Each day presented new challenges and unexpected situations that required on-the-spot decision-making and adaptation.

Yet, amidst the initial shock and confusion, I gradually embraced the fact that it was okay not to have all the answers. Parenthood is a journey of discovery, where learning unfolds alongside the growth of the child. I learned to trust my instincts and seek guidance when needed, whether from experienced parents, healthcare professionals, or support networks.

With time, patience, and an open mind, I began to find my footing as a parent. The experience of raising my child became less about adhering to a rigid plan and more about fostering a nurturing environment where love, care, and flexibility thrived. I came to understand that being a parent meant continuously adapting, learning, and growing alongside my child, rather than attempting to possess all the answers from the start.

In retrospect, while my initial confidence may have been tested, the journey of discovering parenthood from scratch allowed me to embrace the beauty of the unknown. It taught me resilience, humility, and the invaluable lesson that love, and dedication are the strongest foundations for navigating the uncharted territory of caring for a newborn.

I leaned on my family and friends for guidance but there are a lot of things that aren't openly discussed, especially if you don't outright ask, which I didn't. Postpartum was mentioned in a few doctor's visits but within my inner circle, it was rarely talked about. So, when I had my experience with postpartum, I honestly didn't realize it until way after the fact, with me reflecting on things. My experience with postpartum wasn't me having ill feelings towards my baby at all. My issue was with the demands of life and how our current society isn't tailored for moms and taking my frustrations out on my child's father. I created a lot of distance because I wasn't getting the responses I wanted. I felt alone. But, looking back, it was mostly my doing as I created the distance.

The six weeks of maternity leave wasn't enough time to confidently put my child's life, health, and well-being in someone else's hands. I barely knew my kid at this point. We had a schedule but with the days passing and that maternity leave slowly coming to an end, our schedule was about to get shaken up. I was going back to work on a different schedule than before, 6am to 4pm!

The transition of returning to the office after the blissful period of maternity leave was, without a doubt, an ordeal for me. Stepping back into the workplace, I felt like an entirely new person, grappling with a mixture of emotions and challenges. While my return was met with warmth and acceptance from colleagues, I couldn't help but feel a profound sense of awkwardness within myself. I didn't want to be there.

Ah, the notorious pregnancy brain symptom came as a surprise to me as I returned to work. It's a phenomenon that I personally experienced and can wholeheartedly attest to its challenges upon returning to work. Pregnancy brain is a real consequence of the fluctuating hormones that occur during pregnancy, which can impact the functioning of neurons in the brain, leading to various cognitive difficulties such as memory issues, absent-mindedness, and poor concentration. Let me tell you, I forgot a whole lot of stuff. The simple task of remembering my passwords and navigating through what I thought were familiar systems and accounts had become distant during my time away. This sudden lapse in memory only magnified my lack of confidence, as I questioned my ability to perform at the same level of efficiency as before. The feeling of being out of sync with the demands of my job weighed heavily on my shoulders, and I despised the sense of inadequacy.

In my role at the time as Transportation Operations Manager, I developed the ability to memorize our driver's schedules with just a single glance. However, after giving birth to my son, it was a completely different story. I struggled to recall even the basic details, such as the names of the drivers, let alone their intricate schedules. This went on for months, leaving me feeling frustrated and disheartened. It was truly disconcerting to witness the stark contrast between my pre-pregnancy cognitive abilities and the challenges I faced during this period.

To mitigate the effects of pregnancy brain, I eventually started taking a DHA supplement, which is known to promote brain development, in addition to my postnatal vitamins. Over time, I noticed slight improvements in my memory and cognitive function. However, I still grappled with difficulties in remembering passwords and tasks, which made me feel like a mere shell of my former self. Many aspects of my job that were once second nature now required me to relearn them, and it was an arduous process.

The impact of pregnancy brain on my daily life was far-reaching and went beyond what I initially anticipated. The struggles and cognitive impairments caused by pregnancy brain were real and profound. It was a humbling reminder of the immense changes and sacrifices that come with the journey of giving birth and motherhood.

While the effects of pregnancy brain can vary from person to person, it's important to acknowledge and validate the challenges it presents. Taking care of oneself through proper nutrition, including supplements like DHA, and seeking support from loved ones and colleagues can help alleviate some of the difficulties associated with pregnancy brain. Remember, it's a temporary phase, and with time, patience, and self-compassion, cognitive function typically returns to normal.

Another phenomenon that I personally experienced as a new mother was the occurrence of phantom cries with my son. It seemed that no matter how carefully I laid him down for a nap and ensured that he was peacefully asleep before stepping into the shower, I would still perceive the sound of his crying. It became a constant occurrence, causing me to abruptly halt my shower and rush to check on him, only to find him peacefully snoozing, undisturbed.

The phantom cries were both perplexing and disorienting. They played tricks on my mind, making me question my own hearing and perception. Reflecting on this experience, I realized that these phantom cries were not merely a result of my own overactive imagination or irrational fears. Rather, they were a testament to the deep instinctual connection that exists between a mother and her child. The profound responsibility and love we feel for our little ones can create an almost hypersensitivity to their needs, even in the absence of any actual distress signals.

I opted to breastfeed my son. So, when I went back to work, I required a pumping room. I've heard of some moms being embarrassed by the need and being self-conscious about people knowing why they may be away from their desks or workstation. I wasn't embarrassed at all. Personally, pumping was the only thing I was confident about at the time. I work in a male-dominated industry, and the day I came back was when they learned the importance of my new requirement.

I was fortunate to have been provided with a clean and secure location to pump my breast milk, which I lovingly referred to as my "liquid gold." In many ways, these pumping breaks became my personal sanctuary amidst the challenges of balancing work and motherhood. I likened these breaks to the common practice of taking smoke breaks, using it as a discreet cover for my pumping sessions. If anyone inquired, I would casually mention that I was going for a smoke break (with a laugh), concealing my intentions by carrying my bookbag filled with all the necessary pumping equipment.

Religiously, I adhered to my pumping breaks, considering them an essential commitment to my child's well-being. Pumping became a respite that brought solace and tranquility. In those moments of solitude, I felt a heightened sense of accomplishment and validation. Producing my son's meal for the next day gave me a deep-rooted belief that I was doing something right as a mother. During those precious moments, I found myself alone, surrounded by peace. The rhythmic sound of the breast pump, accompanied by the knowledge that I was nurturing my child's health, provided a powerful antidote to the negativity and doubt that often overcame me. It was as if, in those brief interludes, everything else faded away, and I felt an immense connection to my role as a mother.

Pumping allowed me to create a tangible representation of my love and dedication to my child. With each precious drop of breast milk, I knew that I was providing him with vital nourishment, tailored specifically to his needs. This awareness filled me with a sense of fulfillment and reassurance, washing away any doubts or insecurities. The sense of purpose and accomplishment I felt during those moments helped me navigate the challenges of motherhood with renewed vigor and a deep sense of pride.

I struggled with feeling a major sense of guilt for having to put my newborn in daycare six weeks after he was born. My mom and sister expressed their disdain for him being out of my care so soon and that weighed on me as well. My family was in New Jersey, and I was living in Georgia. I was questioning my decision-making for moving so far as I would have had more help in New Jersey. I would've even possibly avoided enrolling my son in childcare altogether.

I can say the facility I enrolled my son in helped a lot with my feelings. We received regular updates regarding feedings and pictures throughout the day, which helped put us both at ease. I'm not going to lie, at first, I stalked the app for updates on my baby.

Guilt is a part of postpartum that isn't spoken about much. I felt like I was a new person, and the looming guilt made me less confident than before. Not to mention having to reacquaint myself to my body. Everything was so different. I was a mom now. I've never had that title before, and I had to define what that would mean to me. I felt that I needed to navigate life differently because of the life I am responsible for, on top of redefining who I was as an individual.

I also ended up having negative feelings toward myself for not having a better option. I questioned myself extensively, and asked myself why I didn't plan better for his arrival. I remember telling myself I should have saved more to be able to afford to be out of work for an extended period of time. My thoughts got the best of me some days. I would vent to my best friend, and she would let me know that my thoughts were unrealistic knowing my prior situation. Realistic expectations went out the window in my mind. In my mind, I should have found a way to do whatever was needed to afford me more time with my son. In the moment of my postpartum, I didn't realize the unrealistic expectations and unnecessary pressure I was applying to myself.

I had some struggles within my relationship due to postpartum. I just didn't feel like my son's father was someone I could vent to, and he wouldn't understand what I was feeling at the time. Truthfully speaking, he was going through his own form of postpartum himself (men have feelings too). But his feelings aside, he was always the voice of reason that I wasn't really looking to hear from. I wanted my feelings to be validated and he always met me with solutions. I can appreciate that aspect now, but that was the last thing I wanted to hear during my postpartum phase. I'm sure it was difficult for him to navigate. He was just being himself, solution-based, and in my moment of postpartum, I just wanted to complain and be heard.

The postpartum period brings about significant changes to our bodies, self-esteem, and overall environment. It can be a time of vulnerability and adjustment, where our pride and ego sometimes hinder us from accepting much needed help. However, I want to emphasize the importance of embracing assistance during this crucial phase. When someone offers to lend a hand, whether it's to cook meals or even drop off prepared meals, help with household chores, or assist with the baby, don't hesitate to accept their support.

Allow yourself to benefit from these acts of kindness. Utilize the opportunity to indulge in self-care activities that rejuvenate your mind and body. Take that relaxing bath or shower you've been longing for, find solace in meditation, immerse yourself in a good book, or simply take a break and do nothing at all. Knowing that someone is present, specifically to care for your baby while you take a moment for yourself, can grant you a sense of relaxation and peace of mind.

Remember, accepting help does not make you weak or incapable. Rather, it acknowledges the fact that being a new parent is an immense responsibility, and it's perfectly okay to lean on others during this transformative period. By allowing others to lend a helping hand, you can focus on your own well-being, recharge, and ultimately become a better parent for your little one. So, set aside any reservations and embrace the assistance that comes your way – it's a gift that can make a world of difference in your postpartum journey.

As new mothers, many of us harbor a strong desire to prove to ourselves and others that we are capable of handling everything on our own. We often hesitate to accept help or support, fearing that it may undermine our sense of independence or competence. However, it's important to recognize that there will come a time when our babies grow older, and the calls asking if we need assistance diminish.

In those moments, we will have ample opportunity to demonstrate our ability to handle everything independently. But during the early stages of motherhood, it's crucial to give ourselves permission to accept help, take breaks, and grant ourselves grace. The journey of motherhood is demanding, both physically and emotionally, and we must prioritize self-care and well-being.

So, if you find yourself experiencing anything from phantom cries to feeling the weight of the world on your shoulders, remember that accepting help is not a sign of weakness but an acknowledgment of the shared responsibility in caring for a child. Give yourself the freedom to take a break, ask for support, and to extend yourself the same compassion and understanding that you offer to your little one. Embracing help and giving yourself grace will ultimately make you a happier, more fulfilled, and more resilient mother.

Chapter 11

Finding Self

Shana Middleton

Imagine being in college and getting pregnant. Then, after having your baby your mom says "your life is over, it's all about the baby now!" What do you do? Of course, You listen to the person that's guided you all of your life. You put yourself on the back burner and you make it all about the baby.

It was the start of my junior year of college, and I had big plans that year. My goal after college was to work for ESPN and to create my very own sports magazine. I had it all planned out. That summer I wanted to get an internship at ESPN or any other media outlet that would give me the experience that I needed. I was looking forward to really putting myself out there, stepping out of my comfort zone and living the life that I dreamed of. Little did I know my life was about to change drastically. During my sophomore year I started dating my high school crush. We were attending the same college and finally became a couple. When junior year came in, we went through some challenges but we were able to bounce back from it. Then, something unexpected happened I became pregnant!!

This was not how my life was supposed to go. I had plans and this was not a part of it. I was pregnant and scared. Will I still be able to do everything I planned? Would I still be able to stay and finish college? So many thoughts were going through my mind. What was I going to do? I decided that I was going to keep my baby. Even though our parents would be upset, I knew they would support us. I knew the road ahead wasn't going to be easy, but I could get through it.

I remember giving birth to my son and looking into his beautiful, big, brown eyes and thinking "what am I supposed to do now?" My mom's voice was in the back of my mind, "it's not about you anymore." Immediately, I started to make changes to accommodate this new life.

I had my son the week before exams. I had to contact all of my professors and hope they would let me reschedule and take my exams later. My senior year was coming up, and I was determined to graduate on time. I moved back home, scheduled all of my classes two days a week and drove back and forth to school. So many changes, and this was definitely not how I pictured spending my senior year of college. I wasn't thinking about what I wanted, but what would work for my son.

My senior year came and it was hard. However, there were some positive aspects that made it easier: I had amazing support from my family and my son's father's family, I lived with my mom and didn't have to work, and my mom assisted me financially. I didn't have to worry about childcare. My son's paternal grandmother took care of him for me. She offered me the opportunity to leave my son at home with her and return to school and enjoy my senior year. However, my mom told me 'No'. She told me that my son was my responsibility, and I agreed with her that I couldn't leave my baby. I was attached to him, the offer was tempting, but I couldn't do it.

My son's father didn't move back home our senior year like I did, but I didn't expect him to. Over time, I started to develop some resentment towards him. He was a very involved father but I felt like he was still able to enjoy college life and I couldn't. I was only at school two days a week for class. There was so much happening on campus that I wanted to be involved in. I wanted to hang out with my friends and my new sorority sisters, but I had a new baby waiting for me at home. I would hang out as much as I could then go back home. My son's grandmother would tell me that I didn't have to rush back, but I felt like I did. When I would pick up my son, seeing his little face eased my disappointment of having to leave school. I realized there was a part of me that honestly felt like I didn't deserve to enjoy myself.

I was raised in a Christian home, and I had committed a sin and got pregnant out of wedlock. No one told me this, but in my mind I felt like not being able to enjoy myself and live the life I really wanted was my punishment. I didn't know what it meant to balance my personal life and motherhood, and during that time I didn't have anyone I felt comfortable talking to or someone to tell me it was okay to live my life and be a great mother. In my mind, the definition of a great mother was 100% sacrifice, and sacrificing who I was and who I wanted to become was everything to my son.

Senior year was coming to an end, and I was so excited. I worked hard and would be graduating on time with honors. I almost felt a sense of redemption. I had gotten pregnant, but I made it!! One of my professors offered me an amazing opportunity to move to another state and attend graduate school, which was something I wanted to do. He even encouraged me to take my son with me, but I was too scared. He was the first person that told me I could have my son and still live my life. There was a part of me that believed him and really wanted this, but there was also a part of me that didn't think I would have the support of my family. I didn't take the offer and I also never told my family about it. After graduation, I took a job that I didn't want, but it was best for my situation. For the next few years, every decision I made was made with my son in mind first. Now, you might be thinking "what's wrong with that, that is what a good mother does." You're right, that is what a good mother does, but a good mother first takes care of herself, and for many years I failed to do that.

As time went on my son's father and I had many ups and downs and eventually ended our relationship. He and his family still played a major part in our son's life. It took some time but we rebuilt our friendship and became amazing co-parents.

I had another son and fell deeper into being their mom and continued to lose who I was. I started to date and men would ask me what I enjoy doing, and I couldn't answer them without saying something about my sons. They would ask, "what do you enjoy doing by yourself?" My mind would go blank, and I had no answer. I couldn't answer them and there was a part of me that was slightly offended that they would ask. I didn't know who Shana was anymore, I only knew "the boy's mom." In certain situations I would only introduce myself as their mom and wouldn't even say my own name...SHANA.

When the boys started school, I was determined to be "that mom." The mom that was on the PTA, the mom that would send snacks to school, the mom that would volunteer, the mom that school could count on. Again, what's wrong with that? Nothing at all, but all of the plans that I was making for my life didn't involve me. I was convinced that being a good mother was being 100% devoted to my children and them only. That's what I saw as a child, I was raised by a single mom and now that's what I was. I wanted to make sure they had a great childhood, that even when I struggled they would never know. I wanted to give them experiences and to travel like I did as a child. I barely can remember a time that I wasn't with my mom besides her going to work. That was the example I saw my entire life. My mom worked hard to provide for my sister and me, sometimes working two jobs. It was always my mom, my sister and me. Now, it was just me and my boys.

I was working in education, and slowly trying to figure out what I really wanted to do. Working in the school system just like my mother and sister provided me with good benefits and a schedule to fit the needs of my kids, but it was never on my list of careers. Something inside of me was starting to wake up. I wanted more, I was starting to think about some of the things I wanted to accomplish and if they were still possible. First on the list was getting my Master's Degree, and working for the school made me think I could be a teacher. I could take online classes which meant I didn't need a babysitter for my children. So, I started working on my Master's in Education, but that didn't last long. I decided that wasn't for me. It was hard for me to figure out what I wanted because I didn't know who I was anymore. I didn't know what I liked to do, and I needed to figure that out first.

Figuring out what I wanted to do with my life proved to be harder than expected. I still loved journalism and still dreamed of working in that field. However, I knew that working in television or radio would mean long hours. I put that thought to the side. I didn't even ask my family if they would help me. I didn't want to be a burden, so I buried that dream. I put getting my master's on the back burner also and enrolled in a Medical and Billing program. That didn't last long either. I was doing really well in the program but it still wasn't enough, and I still didn't know what I wanted to do. Working with the students at the school I started to realize that I enjoyed being a mentor. That led me back to working on my Master's degree to become a Guidance Counselor. I started the program and was excited, but like everything else the excitement didn't last long. I would tell other friends in education what I wanted to do and they would say, "Guidance counselors? Don't do that." I just took what they said, and once again quit the program.

I bounced around the school system working in various positions, one being teaching journalism at a Middle School. I was finally using my degree, and I was enjoying it. But, there was still something missing. I enrolled to work on my Master's again, and this time I knew exactly what I wanted to major in: Human Services. I was slowly finding myself and learning I enjoyed helping people. That's what I enjoyed doing and was trying to find a job where I could do that. I got a job doing exactly what I wanted to do: working with a non profit organization as a Family Navigator. My job was helping people gain access to resources they needed for their families. I loved this job, and I learned so much as I helped so many people. However, this job was grant funded and I needed to figure out what my next move would be.

I was able to find another job where I worked with low income families, helping them get their children in school. I was also responsible for helping those parents enroll in school, get food if they needed it, and get toys for their kids during the holidays. I loved my job, and looked forward to getting up everyday and going to work. I was able to finish my Master's and checked that off my list. I was finding myself more and more. I even discovered a passion for making natural skincare products and started my own business. Serving people brought me so much joy that I never knew existed outside of my children. I was helping people at my job, and in my personal life I was making products that my customers actually loved while growing my business as well. I was starting to see that having my own life outside of my children was possible, and I was finding the balance.

An opportunity for growth presented itself within my company, and it would mean more money for my family. So, I took it. At that time in my life, any increase in salary was appealing to me. I interviewed for the position, and was offered the job. I was so excited. I knew I was going to miss my coworkers, the students and most importantly the parents that I had built a relationship with. However, the chance to make more money as a single parent was too tempting. Unfortunately, once I got in that position I realized that I was no longer working with families. This new position took me away from that and I was miserable. I didn't take into account that this job would be pulling me away from serving people, which was something I grew to love. I needed to find my way back to working with people. I finally realized what I loved doing, outside of being with my children, and I needed to find my way back to it.

I really loved making my products and creating formulas for new products. I wanted to learn more. I really felt connected to this craft and felt like I could take it further and grow it into a bigger business. Getting my esthetician license seemed like the path to take, even though that meant I would have to take classes in person. Could I leave my kids five nights a week for the next eight months? Would my mother help me? For the past fifteen years, I put myself on the back burner. Everything that I wanted to do I would always put it aside. I decided this time it was time to do something for me. For the first time, instead of assuming my family wouldn't help me I sat down and spoke to my mom about how I felt about my job. I told her how unhappy I was and that I wanted to quit. She supported me 100%!! I enrolled in esthetics school, and because of the pandemic I only had in person classes a couple days a week. Things were falling into place, and I was doing something that I wanted to do. I was doing something for me. For once, I thought about myself first.

That old saying "you can't pour from an empty cup," is very true. For years, I tried to do that, I would shrink myself and put my needs aside because I thought that made me a great mother. When I had my oldest son and my mom told me that my life was over, I knew she meant well. That was the life that she lived. I don't know what my mom's dreams were and if she ever got to accomplish them. All I saw was a hard-working woman that made sure her girls were taken care of, when I became a mom I strived to be that for my boys. Fortunately, I found a way to be that mom and to follow my dreams. While I didn't get to work for ESPN or create my magazine, I did find my passion for helping people and now I get to do that for a living. I am now a Licensed Esthetician and the owner of my own spa.

To my amazing sons, when you read this please know that the two of you are the best parts of my life. Everything I do is for the two of you; even putting myself first sometimes. If I try to pour from an empty cup nothing will come out, and I never want to pour nothingness into you guys. In order for me to be the best version of myself and pour positivity into both of you, I have to make sure my cup is filled. Every decision I've made since the two of you were born I would do it all over again. I don't regret anything because I am a firm believer that what is meant to be will be. I found my way to my passion and now you can witness your mom living her dreams. I want the two of you to do the same. Live your life always!!

To my Mother, ever since high school when I'm asked who is the person that I admire the most it is always you. I'm often asked how I can work, maintain a household and take care of two kids by myself. My answer is, "I don't know any other way. I saw my mom do it and I followed in her footsteps." Thank you for instilling in me hard work. Anything I want in life I am willing to work hard for it. For that I am forever grateful to you.

To the person reading this, I hope that you read this and know that you can have the life you want and be the best parent at the same time. The guilt will always be there and the feeling of selfishness will always be there. When you are happy and living in your purpose that is what will make you not only a great parent, but a great person. Live your life to the fullest and go after your dreams. Hopefully, you will be able to instill the same mindset in your children to be able to one day watch them do the same.

Chapter 12

Second Time Around

Luwanna Randle

Hey Girlies,

It's me, Lu, your girl.

The title of this chapter could not have been a better title chosen for me and my experience of becoming a mother. I can't speak for anyone else, but having a second kid with almost eleven years difference was such an eye-opening experience. This time, the journey of motherhood dealt with embracing the growing pains, self-awareness and learning to deal with things the first time around. Things I thought I knew didn't apply the second time around, and things I thought I had dealt with came rushing back to the surface again. I went from a 17-year-old girl raising a little one with almost nothing to being married and having a second baby. Up until my second pregnancy, I thought I was healed and had worked through my personal pregnancy trauma. I thought I was thriving out here. But, if I'm honest, it's more like I stuffed those experiences so far down. I made a promise to myself that it would never happen again if I could do anything about it.

I had my first daughter at the age of seventeen. Like many teenage pregnancy stories, it was one of the hardest things I had ever encountered in my life.

Life before pregnancy, I was described as the "quiet kid", or in today's terminology, an introvert. I had good grades, kept to myself, and never really felt like I belonged to any one particular group. For the most part, people didn't bother to engage with me, and in return I felt the same. To add to the pot, I'm the middle child growing up on the east side of Detroit. So, becoming pregnant automatically thrust me in the spotlight in a way I was totally unprepared for and would have a life-lasting impression. As far as becoming pregnant physically is concerned, there were no complications at all. For me, there was no morning sickness, no swelling feet, or any signs of slowing down in that regard. My woes came from the ridicule, gossip and people who were trying to be sympathetic with statements like, "I understand what you are going through, girl". The reality was they had never really intended to get to know me before this occurrence. Like most teenage relationships, mine didn't last with my daughter's father, which added another layer in having to deal with postpartum depression alone. Looking back, that "Monster" showed up in a way that almost took me out. I became depressed and felt undesirable, I had constant headaches, little to no sleep, and I lost so much weight that I weighed less than before getting pregnant. I was emotional and lacked focus on life including the baby. But, to anyone looking, I was the most well-adjusted teenage mom you could meet.

After looking at my baby girl's face and thinking over all the things I endured in my childhood, I could not let postpartum defeat me. Those thoughts gave me a sense of urgency to change our circumstance. So, I just tucked those emotions deep down and promised to give me and mine better, more and different. I made a vow to keep my focus on getting us out of poverty, and to not have any more kids unless I truly loved the person, was financially able to care for them, and I loved myself. I kept that vow and remained steadfast to seeing the change in my situation. What's funny is, when God calls you to more, He will use your situation to purge things out of you for the better.

I joined the military to build financial stability, went back to school (twice), met a great guy, had people in my circle who really cared about me, and I loved the body I was in. Life was great!

In 2021, I find myself finishing school, landing a great new job, which uproots us a few hundred miles from our previous residence, and we find out we are expecting our baby. What started out as this new excitement to do it all over again but better, slowly started to unravel the things I needed to deal with. Like most pregnancies, I dealt with morning sickness in full force. I became extremely self-conscious of how I would look past eight months. Let's face it, I'm not a pretty pregnant lady past eight months. But, what really started the emotional roller coaster was when my eleven-year-old began to ask questions. There was nothing abnormal about her asking questions. The problem was the fact that I couldn't remember anything before her first birthday due to postpartum depression. I would tear up whenever we would talk because I realized I had blocked out those months.

But that also meant I had blocked out memories of her as well. I didn't have the heart to tell her "I don't remember". So, I lied because it felt better than the truth in my eyes. Then, as soon as I got over that hurdle, issues began to surface with my husband, who was a first-time parent.

Although we were raising my first child together, I realized quickly that I still had some independent woman traits lingering in the background. I dealt with disappointment in the past and had to go through my pregnancy alone. So, it took a while to register that I wasn't alone this time, and my husband and father of our child deserves to be filled in on all the details concerning our baby. I didn't want to cheat him out of the experience.

I really struggled with the me who was used to being independent, and the woman I wanted to be. I would even try doing things on my own and would be extremely exhausted. Then, I wouldn't want my husband to rub on my belly, because of my insecurities and need to know if he still felt me desirable. At one point, I started to question whether he would even love me once I was no longer the small woman I was when we got together.

Finally, after a lot of emotional breakdowns, and a lot of random crying spells, my husband sat me down and suggested that I might find help in therapy. After our heartfelt conversation, I called my sister, who was going to therapy and had shared her experience with me, and asked for advice. The funny thing is, when I did ask her, she mentioned there was another therapist at the office she thought would be a great match for me due to our similar backgrounds. A session was scheduled, and I was ready to go. Getting my life back on track didn't happen overnight. But, over time, I finally got the chance to unpack my baggage. For a long time, I felt like I was unraveling like a tissue roll being forcefully pull by a two-year old.

I learned to lean into the help offered by those who love me. I stopped being distant towards my husband and let him rub and touch my belly, even when I felt uncomfortable. Whether I could do it or not, I let him put on my shoes, and when it came time to make dinner, I sat in the chair and gave instructions for meal preparation. I learned that even though I didn't remember all the details of my oldest daughter's younger years, it didn't mean I was a bad mom, or I loved her any less. Things were finally getting better.

Eventually, February 2022 arrived and Miss Renee with it. Having the opportunity to work out my past prepared me for the events that would follow. During labor, I had an emergency C-section that placed the baby in the NICU and left me more dependent on my husband than I had anticipated. The love and patience my husband showed during this time made a lasting impression on my heart. I had to depend on him in ways I would not have been able to receive had I not unpacked my past trauma. That period of time in our marriage made a lasting impact on me that I will forever store in my heart.

I continually thank and praise You, God!

I have a new understanding of Romans 8:28 - And we know that all things work together for good to them that love God, to them who are the called according to his purpose.

If I could leave you with something: even if you need to repeat the task again, that does not mean God left you to do it alone. Find your Help, Create your Support and Be an Advocate for yourself!

Much Love, LuWanna

Chapter 13

Postpartum with Multiple
Kelly Morris-Jordan

How do I start this off? Well, let me just start from the beginning by introducing myself, My name is Kelly. I am happily married and a mother to two girls and two boys for which I am so grateful. Often, as we watch parents begin their journey into parenthood, all we see is the glitz and glamour. What we sometimes forget is that being a parent, especially being a mother, is such a huge and demanding challenge.

What I believe makes my story so unique is me having postpartum depression added to the childhood traumas I was already trying to deal with. It was not only difficult, but it was one of the worst experiences in my life. I wanted what I never had for my children: to raise them in a loving two-parent household. But, who knew that when I decided to go on this journey, I would have such negative and harmful thoughts. I never knew that postpartum was a thing until I gave birth.

When my first child was born, my husband was away starting his career in the Marine Corps. So, when it was time for me to give birth, I felt as if I was alone with my husband being away. What made matters worse was me being ignorant of postpartum depression. It was never discussed in my family. I am not sure that anyone in my family truly knew anything about postpartum depression. But, you would think that once you have a child, you would inform your doctor about what you are feeling. Well, the guilt will cause you to keep it to yourself. You will think twice about expressing your feelings to your husband or friends. You don't want them to think you are out of your mind. So, you just tell yourself "Girl this is just a phase, get over it, you will be fine, and you are about to be a mom for the first time. So, you tell yourself you're just being fearful and thinking of all the bad experiences others have told you about their labor".

I truly and honestly thought after having my first born that I was going to always be happy. Never have I ever thought otherwise. After eight hours of labor, she was finally in my arms, and I was so happy. I could not find the words to express how I felt holding this tiny human that I created, incubated, carried, and birthed. She was such a beautiful baby. I looked deep into her eyes and held her tiny body close to my chest as she stared back at me. I saw this mini version of me, and suddenly all the feelings of panic and fear just started to go away.

Three weeks after giving birth, I am a complete mess. I couldn't sleep throughout the night because my baby girl was not sleeping at night. I hardly had time for anything. I felt overwhelmed, subconscious because I had a c-section, and I was in so much pain. To top it off, I was being hit with so many mixed emotions, and had no clue what was going on with me.

A few weeks after our daughter was born, my husband came home from training. I was so excited because this was his first time ever meeting her. I was over the moon happy for him. Especially, because she was our first born. As excited as I was, I also just wanted some quiet "me time." I craved peace and sleep, and would've been happy for even a few hours. But, because I was breastfeeding, I felt I needed to always be around her. This made it difficult to get any time to myself. I didn't know any better. I thought I couldn't have time to myself because I was a mom.

As I was battling these new emotions alone, I began to realize I was not properly nourishing my body. After giving birth, I gained so much weight that it made me feel undesirable and unattractive. Being alone fueled my negative thoughts (my husband ended up only being home for a few weeks before being shipped back out to his new duty station out of the country).

Two years went by, and I noticed the disconnect with my baby. I was always crying myself to sleep hoping that things would get better. But, it didn't because I still wasn't ready to face the fact that I needed help.

We eventually decided to have another baby. When my second girl was born, I could not stand to look at her, and my husband was leaving again after three weeks. I asked myself "Why did I do this to myself again?" I had another c-section when I did not fully recover from my first pregnancy. As a mom, I felt I should not be saying things like this, and I should not have these feelings. Right?!

Adding two kids to the mix and not knowing what to expect was tough. Things had gotten so bad that I would leave my kids in another room crying because I could not handle the pressures of being a mom. I didn't recognize the woman in the mirror anymore. My body changed so much, as well as my focus. Everything had to be about the babies and my husband's needs.

My husband started to notice some things and tried to help as much as he could by taking care of the girls' needs in order for me to rest. But, as crazy as it sounds, I was also so protective of them that I didn't even want him to interfere or be around. My husband made many attempts to help wherever he could, but was unsuccessful. There were times he didn't really know what to do. I honestly believe I was being selfish and so inconsiderate of his feelings. I also doubted him being a good father to our children. All of this was out of character for me.

I remember going to my primary doctor and having to fill out the postpartum questionnaire. It seemed like the floodgates opened. I told my doctor I felt worthless, always tired and sluggish, not myself, and I found myself sleeping all the time. I even admitted to having suicidal thoughts. At this point, I really did hate being a mom. This was the hardest thing in the world to acknowledge. I felt as if evil spirits were taking over me. As I am explaining my feelings to my doctor, she informs me that what I was experiencing was postpartum depression. She gave me a brochure on it and quickly gave me a prescription for this drug called Zoloft. It was new at the time. Well, at least it was new to me.

When I would take it, I would feel worse than I did without it. It made me very drowsy and even sadder. I did not like the way I felt. So, I completely took myself off it and refused to ask for anything else. I felt like my doctor was not helping at all. It felt as if she was quick to prescribe medications. I was not looking for a prescription, I was looking for answers as to why I felt the way I did and how to cope. After my experience with postpartum depression, I honestly believe there should be something in place for all mothers to receive free therapy sessions right after they give birth.

I told myself, before trying another prescription, it would be a good idea for me to find myself. That's what I thought I needed. A couple of months before my husband left the Marine Corps., which was a topic of many heated discussion between us, we agreed on me staying home full-time. But eventually, I decided I needed to go back to work. I didn't care what type of job it was as long as it fit with me working around my girls. With everything I was feeling and going through, I still was not giving up. I wanted to be the best mother I could be, and I also did not want to be separated from them. I was so scared to leave my husband with them. It had nothing to do with trusting him, it was me being extremely conflicted about not being there for my kids. I was still dealing with my negative thoughts and other postpartum depression symptoms.

Eventually, I found a part time job and went back to work. This period in my journey through motherhood and postpartum depression was hard, but I felt some ease. Even though it may have been temporary. I still faced challenges because the hours I worked were difficult. I would leave before my girl's bedtime just to get home after three a.m. I would only get a few hours of sleep and would have to get up in the morning to take care of the girls. On the days where I was not working, I still felt extremely alone and overwhelmed. After my husband left the service, he was working full time, but also going to school for his bachelor's degree. There was even a time where he found a second part time job to help ends meet.

Do not get me wrong, I love my husband for everything he has done to provide for us. But in these early years of our marriage and life as parents, I needed him with me the most. My thoughts would have me feeling like he wasn't there and didn't care. I trust and love my husband and knew he was and is a good father. But, when I was at work, my thoughts would run rampant. There were days when I would come home from those late nights, worried that my husband had fallen asleep and let the girls get into something they weren't suppose to. Children are curious and my girls are no different. They got into stuff, but the postpartum depression and separation anxiety had me thinking the worse.

As time went on, I started to feel good to the point where I would get up and do my hair, makeup, and other fun things with my daughters. I even decided to go back to school. Everything seemed like it was going well. Then suddenly, I started to have pregnancy symptoms again. I went to the store and bought over six different types of pregnancy tests. I was being so extra, in all honestly. But I did not want to be pregnant again. I did not want to deal with the same thoughts I dealt with. Especially, now that I find myself getting back to me. Then again, I wanted to give my husband his first son. He wanted a namesake. I found the courage to take the pregnancy tests. Of course, the tests came back positive. I was pregnant with our third child. We were both excited about this unexpected news, even though we really weren't expecting to have another child. We both thought that we were not financially ready to have another one.

I decided to find a new OB/GYN just to get confirmation. During the examination, the doctor gets silent. I asked her if there was something wrong, and that's when she told me she couldn't find a baby to confirm my pregnancy. I go into panic mode because she did not have any answers to give me. Then, she leaves the room, which only exacerbated the panic and worry I was feeling. When she finally comes back, she explains the situation. She tells me that she was not able to find my baby, but it looks as if he was in my tubes. My OB/GYN also told me that I may have to have surgery to terminate my pregnancy.

I was at a loss of words, shaking, hyperventilating, and crying. But something told me to relax and ask if another ultrasound could be done. The doctor agreed and proceeded to take another look. Sure enough, he was not in my tubes, but hiding behind a layer of fat. I was so relieved and excited. For that split second, I noticed the emotions and feelings that were washing over me. Many of them were the same ones I felt after my girls were born. This pregnancy was different because of the setbacks and scares as well as me working this time.

At my next appointment, I was still shaken and realized I was really uncomfortable with my doctor. But, I didn't want to go through the hassle of changing doctors. I should've followed my first mind, but I decided to just deal with it. She does another ultrasound and then, proceeds to check my weight. I can't remember her exact words, but she said something along the lines of me being too fat. I remember saying to myself, "that wasn't professional". Being a woman who is already curvy, there was no way I thought that I had to be one hundred and twenty pounds to have a baby. But, because of me already dealing with body issues all my life, I was offended and quickly switched doctors.

I had my first baby boy in 2016 with ease. He was so beautiful and looked just like me. Then, right after that my last and final baby boy came along via c-section in 2017. I guess he didn't want to share birthday months with is older brother. So, he decided to start "cutting up" on Christmas Eve. He put a lot of stress on my body, but finally arrived on Christmas Day. I call him my miracle baby and my blessing, because he wasn't due to come for another month. On the other hand, I thought God was punishing me. I kept asking myself, "how am I going to do this with four children?" My anxiety was all over the place and I just went deeper and deeper into depression.

The following is a note I wrote during this time of depression: "Currently in the bathroom and I cannot seem to hold it together. You know how you feel like you are not living up to your own standards. I feel like I am not good at anything. Been working hard at work. I feel like my work ethic is finally getting noticed, but I still feel like I am just out of place sometimes. At home I feel like I am failing all the time. Nothing seems right. Nobody can feel this pain that I am fighting every day. It truly hurts. I feel like this time I cannot shake it. I have been trying even on my birthday: I felt okay trying to distract myself by going out somewhere doing something that I love. It has gotten to that point to where I feel like I should just end it. A part of me is saying how selfish it would be on my part if I just do it and get it over with.

There is this little mini voice saying what effect would that have on my children as they get older? Will they ever think of me as a failure because I lost the battle? I guess all I can do is continue to fight even though I feel like my life is worthless. Who knows? I will not be writing like this again. I do hope the Lord can help me and heal me. Until then, I am going to make my family dinner, even though I want to hide under my covers in my bed. You know I should be truly proud of myself for what I have."

It breaks my heart having to see this now, knowing that I had this person in the back of my head telling me I should just give up and not think of the impact it would have had on my children. It could have been a cycle that repeated itself. I finally came to the conclusion that enough was enough when me and my husband got into this huge fight. It was so bad that he ended up saying that he was giving up on us. At this time, he knew what was going on with me, but I still hadn't come to the point of getting help. I gave up and said you know what, let me take myself over the staircase and be done with it. What was traumatizing was that my oldest saw me and she said to me, "Mommy! No! Don't! I love you! I need you!" The words from her moved me and stopped me. Suddenly, I think to myself, "What am I doing? Why do I keep doing this to myself?

I just didn't want to feel pain anymore. I was suffering to the point of even experiencing abdominal pain. I wanted it to stop. My husband held me tight that day and kept reminding me that I have so much to live for and that our children needed me. The next day, shame and guilt set in. I just wanted to hide. So, I literally hid in my closet because I did not want anyone to see me.

My husband did what he said he would. He sent me information on a few therapists, and I called two and left a message for the second one. In my voicemail, I left a detailed message expressing my need for help. A few days later she returned my call and immediately sent me the information she needed from me to get me started with therapy. Since then, I have been going to her every week. We've had some hard sessions, but I know therapy is helping and I will never give up.

Today I can sit here and say, "Wow, I have come a long way!" Life has been a challenge, but it's also been amazing. I want to encourage you to always remember that you can make it through this thing called life. Going through postpartum depression is normal. Don't let anyone tell you that it is not. It has taken me thirty-three years to finally accept help in my life. I am not going to lie to you. It has been a long and hard journey for me. But, I am thriving and pushing through. I realize I am stronger than I give myself credit for. Sharing my story was not easy, but I really hope that it helps another mother to keep fighting. Queen, life is full of blessings. Never give up! Your children deserve to love you the way you love them. Unconditionally.

Chapter 14

Intrusive Thoughts

Jessica N. Monroe

Intrusive Thoughts -

So, what does that mean? An intrusive thought is an unwanted thought, image, impulse or urge that can occur spontaneously or that can be cued by external / internal stimuli.

If you asked me what I wanted to be when I grew up it definitely wasn't a mom. Growing up I had goals and a desire to travel. I watched my mom work so hard at work and at home. She kept our house running with ease, and in my eyes she was perfect. You could say that's when the intrusive thoughts were born: those moments watching my mother keep our house afloat.

Fast forward to 2006, Sam and I found out I was pregnant. All my fears, worries and what-ifs began to brew. One of my first intrusive thoughts was dealing with the challenges of becoming a mom at 18. I wondered if I could be half of the mom that I had growing up. Would I be able to love this baby? What would his life be like? Would our families accept him? How would our lives change? How would our future professional goals change and adjust to having a child? Those nine months flew by, and Cam was born. I quickly realized how fast those thoughts would take over. Within a few hours we became a family of three and we had a lot of things to figure out. My first big concern was about breastfeeding. Because of my young age, I hadn't talked to anyone about the topic. I vividly remember after delivery when the lactation specialist came into the room to help. It was a very overwhelming experience. My lack of experience was evident and I felt like I was being judged. I was worried about what my peers and family would think about me breastfeeding, I wasn't sure if I was going to be able to produce enough to keep him healthy, and all the while, I felt like I couldn't ask for help from anyone. I didn't know another person at the time that chose to breastfeed, and didn't have anyone to talk to. That was my first big letdown. Every time he would cry, I would get so sad. Is this milk enough? What am I doing wrong?

I remember being sad about my thoughts and feelings. It had been a little over two months since I had Cam. I knew I needed to talk to someone. So, I took a leap of faith and went to see a behavior specialist to make sure I was okay. I wanted to make sure my thoughts weren't going to hurt either of us. The shame I felt before going to the appointment was overwhelming. All I remember from the meeting was being told that I was okay. I was told that after having a baby your body's hormone levels are all over the place and that my body needed time to adjust. The specialist said my thoughts were just worries and I was far from any space that she felt I needed any form of medical help. I went home feeling validated. I knew I loved him and that I was doing the best that I could. After the meeting I would find myself giving myself personal pep talks to get through my worries. My pep talks helped with my intrusive thoughts and made me change for the better. Naturally, as Cam got older, my worries started to change. Instead of feeding issues, I worried about how I would raise him. Would me being a young mom hurt him or hold him back? I made it a top priority to make sure he would be healthy, smart, and successful.

Getting married young came with its own intrusive thoughts. But, being pregnant with baby number two just added to the list. I personally feel that after each new baby I would have some form of intrusive thoughts. With baby number two, we were dealing with truly being on our own with two kids for the first time. A brand-new baby, a toddler, and a husband in the military. I felt like we were managing the stress alright. Then a few months go by and it's time for us to prep for my husband's first deployment. The most stressful thing about it was that it was a short notice deployment. I did not feel like I was enough and could handle two small kids all by myself. The sadness quickly took over. The new baby was completely different from Cam. He was needy, and I had a hard time dealing with him crying all the time. It took time to get adjusted and the routine developed slowly. Luckily, as the baby got older, he became more independent and self-soothing. This made caring for two small children easier. I felt like that deployment helped me build confidence in my ability as a mother.

As we became settled with our family and routine a few years later, we decided it was time to add to our family. When we got pregnant with baby number three, life was great. Around 20 weeks we found out that there was a possibility that he would be born with a birth defect. Our OBGYN tried her best to keep us worry free, but it was a lot to take in.

Fast forward to the delivery date…

For a moment, everything was perfect. He had arrived and was crying just as he should. The specialist quickly entered the room to give him a thorough exam and started educating us on how to care for him. During that time, it was a constant battle of what was reality and what my intrusive thoughts wanted me to believe. What we knew was that our sweet baby was born with a cleft lip and palate. We knew that he was healthy but would need surgery soon, and would need a few surgeries throughout his life. We also knew that we had a team of doctors ready to help in any way they could to make our life as "normal" as possible. However, what I was hearing in my head were whispers of mom guilt. What did you do wrong? Did you take enough vitamins?

New feeding woes and worries came along with the challenge of a baby with a cleft lip. I felt a constant need to hide him from the world, worrying about posting and sharing pictures before his lip surgery in fear of judgement from other people. But with time we got the hang of things. The thoughts had less power the more information I had. We got better with each feeding and that started to build confidence in our ability to care for our special little one.

Here I am a mom of three boys and thinking I had everything figured out. We got pregnant with our fourth, and we were thrilled to welcome our first girl. It meant so much to me to have a baby version of myself, and I immediately came up with the perfect delivery plan for my little girl. I knew I wanted to give birth naturally so that when the day came for her to have her own, I would be able to relate to her. After going in for a routine checkup we ended up having to head over to labor and delivery. Something was wrong with her heart rate. We didn't expect that Monday to turn into her birthday. In a little over twenty-five minutes, my world and plans changed. Our baby girl was born, and I was filled with emotions. While I was thankful she was here, I also couldn't help but feel defeated. My birth plan was out of the window, and everything made me cry. I felt like less of a woman for not naturally delivering her. I didn't know just how bad this birth would affect me. I wanted a natural birth, and ended up with having an emergency c-section. I think Sam quickly noticed I was sadder than I had been with our other deliveries. I'm not very good with change. So, when my plans had to shift, I started to beat myself up about the kind of mother I was for my daughter. I just couldn't shake the feeling of guilt and became more depressed after moving a few weeks after her birth. I was sad about everything. I felt like she could feel my sadness. Breastfeeding her was difficult. I started to isolate myself because I just couldn't handle my guilt and sadness. My friends reminded me that I was a great mom even if my plans didn't go as I had hoped. Slowly but surely, I began feeling like myself again.

By the time we had baby number five, our expectations were a little more realistic and flexible when it came to managing a delivery plan. In a perfect world, I would have loved to have a VBAC (vaginal birth after cesarean), but my doctor was upfront with me. He gave us a deadline date and a date for a c-section. What we didn't expect was having a full-size baby in a Neonatal

Intensive Care Unit (NICU). We felt so out of place. We never had a baby in there before, so it came with a lot of intrusive thoughts. While I should have been resting from surgery, I was upstairs sitting with our little one. The mom guilt didn't allow me to see I needed rest, and that it would make things better for both me and baby. When we got home, I struggled with sitting down and resting. I wanted to be the same active mom I was to our other kids before welcoming our baby girl. I felt guilty that I was not enough because I couldn't manage everything on my own. Asking for help was my least favorite thing to do. Sam stepped in and made sure I knew that asking for help wasn't the end of the world. It wasn't going to take anything away from me an awesome mother and wife.

With our last little one the challenges were stacked from beginning to end. The intrusive thoughts that arrived ruined our pregnancy experience. After meeting with our specialist, things seemed so scary. I had preexisting health issues and it was going to make growing our little one that much harder. Guilt and frustration is what I frequently felt. My health stole my joy in our last pregnancy. It felt easier to not acknowledge that I was pregnant, because I didn't want to get attached. I had to focus so much on my health that I wasn't able to enjoy the pregnancy. I knew once we hit twenty weeks we would know if baby number six would be ok. Our nurse begged me to buy something for the baby so we could have some positive reinforcement, but I let all my intrusive "what if" thoughts get in the way. After that ultrasound, so much joy was welcomed. I believe that was the first time during the pregnancy, I left an appointment happy. The confidence that appointment gave me allowed me the chance to relax and let go of most of my "what-ifs". I was so private with the pregnancy that I know to some of our family and friends, it may have felt like I was distant. But, I was trying to protect myself, which led to me having a deeper conservation with my husband about boundaries I created for myself and our family.

By the time baby boy arrived I was in a much better place. I was able to express my fears and concerns without feeling like a burden. I was just blissfully happy about bringing him home to join our tribe. A few weeks after we gave birth I had a decision to make. Our son born with the cleft lip and palate was having a major surgery. I was still recovering from a c-section and we would have to drive to another state for the surgery. It was a big moment for our family as a whole. We were closing on a house, school was starting soon, and we had a brand new baby. Normally we would just figure it out, but this time we decided to ask for help. We were vocal in our need for support. The intrusive thoughts were in my head for sure, but I tried my best to look at the bigger picture. I was worried about not showing up for our older child. I didn't want him to feel left out because of the new baby. But, I knew I needed to rest and heal.

We had a ton of things that we needed to do to prep for buying our new house and leaving our rental. So, we asked for help. That was the biggest blessing in a scary season. Our parents showed up to help with the grandkids while we were away for the surgery, my best friend and her daughter drove up and spent the day during surgery, and all of our family and friends sent cards to our cleft kid. When we arrived back home we felt so loved. The boys were both covered in my love and I didn't miss a moment. Sam made sure me, the newborn, and our son with the cleft lip and palate were taken care of. The intrusive thoughts didn't have power after I realized it was okay to delegate and receive help from others.

Looking back over my pregnancy journeys, I noticed that I have had intrusive thoughts about more than just pregnancy and our deliveries. I tried to focus on being a mom to a new baby, but life was still happening outside of me and the new baby: family time, cleaning the house, dating my spouse, and maintaining friendships. I've had intrusive thoughts about being a military spouse, and I worried about how I would be seen coming into a new spouse group. Being a wife on paper looks easy, but somewhere in the many years and having several kids, life can have you worrying over a lot of small things. Such as, are we making enough time for each other? Do we both feel seen and heard? Making friends every time we move, trying to put together a safe circle for our family, and making time for friends and extended family even came with guilt when I took time away. I worried constantly about the life I expected for our kids early on. Would they be blessed with a tribe to watch them grow? Would Sam and I be enough to manage all the things that our six kids would need?

Most of my intrusive thoughts came during my pregnancies, deliveries, and postpartum. However, there are many other moments in my life that I personally experienced them. As I was writing, I realized how many moments in my life I did not see the light at the end of the tunnel. I also noticed that with time, grace and a routine things got better. I also noticed that no two experiences were the same. Some of them required me to see a specialist and others simply just took time to get better. With pregnancies and deliveries, I feel like we are often told that in six weeks everything is going to be back to normal. That is simply not true for everyone, and that is okay. There are so many factors that can affect that process. The best thing I did was give myself grace. The goal was to stop operating in a space of guilt and "what-ifs". I had to learn that asking for help from either my spouse, family, friends, or associates does not make me weak. I also try to remember well after that magical six-week window, things could use some more time to become manageable.

If only I could tell young Jessica what I know now. I would tell her:

- Communicate with her spouse about her fears and concerns.
- It's okay to ask for help and to delegate.
- Have a conversation about expectations, boundaries, and goals for both you and your husband before and after your pregnancy.
- No matter the delivery outcome with your daughter, you will have a lifetime to forge a bond with her.
- Take more pictures of your son with the cleft lip and palate, you'll miss precious moments if you don't. I know you think you're protecting him but there are better ways. Take the time to educate those who have questions.

After I got older and had a few kids, I began sitting down and having conversations with my mom about motherhood. After a lifetime of thinking that she raised us so perfectly and effortlessly, she began to reveal the reality of her motherhood experience. She opened up about the challenges she faced and the obstacles she had as a mother. What stuck out the most was that she also had intrusive thoughts and overcame them. Whatever the situation, no matter how big or small, she told me she leaned on her faith and the love for her children. She has always wanted the best for us and would do whatever it took to make sure we were okay. Even though we are adults, my mom still shows up for her children as we navigate our own journey as parents. Those talks taught me that even the strongest woman in the world (my mom!) faced difficult times.

My desire is to teach my children (especially my daughters) that intrusive thoughts can come in parenthood. The important thing to note is we all struggle in one way or another, but there are ways to manage it. Give yourself some grace, don't be afraid to ask for help and know that it takes time.

And remember, you're doing a great job!

Conclusion

In this book, you have read stories from breastfeeding, returning to work, body image and many other inspiring journeys. Our hope is that you found love, acceptance, and understanding within these wonderful mommy stories. We would like to leave you with a postpartum prayer and a week's worth of affirmations.

Postpartum Prayer

Father,

Hold my hand through this postpartum journey. I am unsure of what to except during this period, but I know with you I can handle anything. Father, strength my spirit and release the Comforter to bring me peace during the dark times. I want to thank you in advance for the love, community, strength, and joy during this postpartum period.

Postpartum Affirmations

I am a strong woman that knows how to accept help

I am doing an amazing job

I am thankful for my body with all the flaws

I am a woman first, then a mother

I am not alone and there are other mommies who want to support me

I am walking in grace and understanding during this period

I am in love with the new me, she's perfectly imperfect

Postpartum Depression Support

If you feel like you may be experiencing postpartum depression please call your doctor, nurse, midwife, or pediatrician if:

- Your baby blues doesn't go away after 2 weeks
- Symptoms of depression get more and more intense
- Symptoms of depression begin within one year of delivery and last more than 2 weeks
- It is difficult to work or get things done at home
- You cannot care for yourself or your baby (e.g., eating, sleeping, bathing)
- You have thoughts about hurting yourself or your baby

Letter from HIM

Dear Mothers,

You are truly a gift to this world. No one else has the innate capacity to do what you have done nor to be who you are. You are every child's first true love, from that very first cry when they enter the world. You are the phenomenal nurturer who gives tirelessly to ensure that nourishment is provided. You are the comforter that soothes the hurts of life, and the encourager that cheers when no one else is rooting. You are the amazing teacher that provides instruction and guidance for navigating through life.

You provide happiness and jubilation in times of sorrow and sadness. The one who brings peace and a sense of security to the lives of a child. You are the stability and strength of the family structure. The absolute heart of the home that cares for the well-being of all who reside. You are the greatest gift God has bestowed upon this earth; you are unmatched and extraordinary. When times seem tough and unrewarding, know that you are loved and so very appreciated. You are a mother.

Sincerely, Gabriel Collier

Meet the Authors

Naviane Collier

Naviane is a second time author with her inaugural self-published book titled Seek, Know, Plan; centered around personal and professional development for aspiring leaders. Naviane is a Global Training Manager and women's Christian Wellness Coach. She is originally from Detroit, Michigan where her mother currently resides. Naviane received her Master of Science degree in Industrial and Organizational Psychology with a concentration in Leadership Development and Coaching from Walden University. She obtained her Bachelor of Arts degree in Psychology from Benedict College where she met her husband, Gabriel Collier. Naviane and her husband currently live in Houston, Texas where they are first time parents to their son, Roman Collier. Naviane's life mission is to help women go from self-sabotage to self-worth by the Word of God and wellness. She encourages and supports women that are going through the postpartum period. If you're looking for additional support, you can follow Naviane on Instagram (@her_wellness). She's helping women go from self-sabotage to self-worth.

Lexxus Betts Keyes

Lexxus Betts Keyes is a wife and a mother whose foundation begins with her spirituality and walk in faith through Christ. She strives for relentless pursuit of excellence in all her work and encounters. She is a 2017 Graduate at North Carolina Agricultural and Technical State University with a Bachelor's in Biomedical Engineering. She is currently matriculating at the University of North Carolina at Pembroke pursuing her Master's in Business Administration. Lexxus works in the medical device industry as a Global Product Manager in the area of Interventional Cardiology/Radiology. Lexxus has a passion for bridging the healthcare and medicinal gaps for underrepresented persons. Lexxus has her own business in the area of Digital Marketing and Event Management and co-founded a non-profit, Thrive Women's Empowerment, Inc. in 2017. Lexxus in hopes any mothers or mothers-to be reading Words to Her is encouraged by the stories and know that they are not alone. It takes a village to raise a child and we are in hopes to add to your village.

Morgan Taylor-McFadden

Morgan Taylor-McFadden is a dedicated advocate for addressing racial inequity in maternal health, with a strong focus on ensuring quality care and resources for self-identified Black women. Currently serving as the Director for Boston Healthy Start Initiative, a grant-funded program operating under the Boston Public Health Commission, Morgan is deeply committed to reducing disparities in maternal and infant health.

With a remarkable background, Morgan previously held the role of Program Supervisor for the Black Infant Health Program, where she supported and uplifted African American pregnant women in South Central L.A. through social initiatives. Prior to that, she contributed to ABCD Boston from 2013 to 2016, furthering her impact on the community.

Beyond her professional accomplishments, Morgan is a trained birth/postpartum doula and a Yoga Practitioner. Originally from Los Angeles, California, she has called Boston her home for the past nine years, finding fulfillment and purpose in her work within the maternal health field.

For Morgan, this work is not just a job; it is deeply personal. Born premature at a little past 6 months, weighing only 3.3 pounds, her journey in maternal health comes full circle. Drawing inspiration from her lived experiences as a Black mother/birthing person of two young daughters, Isis and Assata, she continues to be driven by her dedication to create a more equitable and supportive maternal healthcare system.

Nigerain Collier

Nigerain Collier was born and raised in Winston- Salem North Carolina as a first generation Liberian American. She attended North Carolina A&T State university where she received her Bachlores in psychology and became a member of Zeta Phi Beta Sorority Inc. There, she met her husband Emanuel, who is a member of her brother fraternity Phi Beta Sigma Fraternity Inc. After college, they got married and both decided to start their family and turn a household of two into a home of three. She gave birth to her baby girl Skylar in 2022. She believes nothing is more important than God, family, and embracing life for everything that it has to offer. If you ask Nigerain she will tell you that pregnancy is beautiful however it is definitely a journey. She believes that every woman, regardless of their birthing process has a story to tell. That is why she wanted to give you a glimpse of her own personal story, reminding you that you are not alone and that all the mamas across the world are in this together.

Dynika Marshall

Dynika Marshall was born and raised in the city of Monroe, Georgia, where she cherishes some of her most precious moments. Dynika is currently an Advisory Manager for KPMG and recently joined the best hood of all, Motherhood! Dynika considers her family as her #1 priority and the upmost important aspect of her life. While maintaining a busy work life and active family, Dynika explored the juggling act of motherhood and decided to put pen to paper. Words To Her is Dynika's first co-author book.

Rodneshia Seals

Rodneshia Seals was born and raised in Atlanta and prides herself on being an original Georgia Peach. Rodneshia values faith, family and friends. Without one of the three, she isn't whole. Faith and love anchors her and she loves spending time with family and friends alike. Rodneshia found a love for journaling and writing poems at a young age and had one of her poems titled "Who am I" published when she was just in the 6th grade.

Quantisha Oliver

Quantisha Oliver was born and raised in Miami Florida. Quantisha enjoys singing and dancing, she is also a mentor for "troubled youth". Quantisha uses her life experience to help children and teens make better life choices and ensure that in all things her mentees put psGod first. Quantisha is a wife and mother. she is also a youth minister at her church United Disciples of Christ Church in Ridgeville, SC. When she's not singing or dancing you can find her writing and spending time with her family making the most out of every moment they share together.

Amber D. Brown-Jones

My Name is Amber D. Brown-Jones. I have served and survived 30 years on this earth. My Husband and I have been married for three years, and we have two wonderful children, Charlie and Dakota. Although I lived under my single mother's roof with my two sisters, my mom had the support of her mom, sisters, and cousins during our upbringing. Having grown up in a small town where everyone knows everyone, I couldn't keep anything hidden. Amid gossip and drama, no one offered guidance where we young ladies most needed it. I was commonly frowned upon and viewed as if I would not make it or make something of myself. "A fast little girl.", as they said, "Hot in the draws.". No one was discussing what was crucial. It was do or die for me, and I had to learn as I progressed. I am always about proving someone wrong who doubts my capabilities. I am a working woman paying a mortgage on my first home while attending college with less than twelve months remaining before I secure and walk away with my Business Bachelor's degree in Project Management. What means the most to me is my mothership. As a mother, I have experienced love and nurturing throughout my life. As an individual, I have experienced suffering and heartache. From such experiences, I have learned that I love my children so much that I wish I never had them.

Mary K. Purnell

Mary Purnell was born and raised on the South Side of Chicago IL. She is extremely family orientated and comes from a close knit family. She is a proud member of the illustrious sorority Alpha Kappa Alpha Sorority Inc. She takes pride in being a mom and balancing a demanding career. With a MS in Corporate Accounting and an MBA in Business Leadership and Management she serves as the Business Services Director for the AAPD. Her determination to succeed is driven by her son and she knows that with hard work and God all things are possible. If she is not working she is spending time with her family, friends and line sisters when life allows them to.

Shana Middleton

Shana Middleton is a native of South Carolina. Growing up, she had a very big imagination and was very creative. She also has a love for reading and would read for hours and hours. She has two sons and when she isn't spending time with them and her family, she runs her own business as a Licensed Esthetician. She also is an Esthetics instructor. Words to Her, is Shana's first book.

Whitney Moody

Whitney was born and raised in New Jersey. She is very family oriented and spends most of her time with her son, nieces, and sisters. She is a transportation professional and a serial entrepreneur in her spare time. She enjoys traveling, has a passion for cooking, and is always working towards her next goal. Words to Her: Postpartum Stories for Mommies is her first take on writing professionally.

Luwanna Randle

Luwanna Randle was born in raised in Detroit but currently reside in Texas. Where spending with her family is the upmost important to next to provide spacing for herself. She loves to try new activities and watching cartoons with her kids. Word to Her: Postpartum Stories for Mommies would be her first time in a publish book.

Kelly Morris-Jordan

Kelly Morris-Jordan was born in 1989 on the South side of Chicago Illinois where she spent most of her life. She was raised mainly by her grandparents. Early in life, she met her husband who served in the military. Due to his military career, they moved to California and stayed after his career ended. Kelly and her husband have four beautiful children by the names Hayden, Leah, Robert Jr., and Tristan. In her spare time, she loves to cook, listen to music, make homemade wine from her own private garden, and spend time with her children and husband. She is currently enrolled in Western Governors University pursuing her bachelor's degree in Healthcare Management. Instagram: @kellymj19

Jessica N. Monroe

Jessica Monroe was born and raised in the Lowcountry of South Carolina. She is a military spouse and mother to six amazing kids. Jessica loves planning, traveling, and all things Disney. After 17 years of being a stay-at-home mom, she's looking forward to this next chapter of her story!

Made in the USA
Monee, IL
10 September 2023